THE
NEW TESTAMENT
LETTERS

The
New Testament Letters

PREFACED AND PARAPHRASED

by

J. W. C. WAND, D.D.

BISHOP OF LONDON
FORMERLY BISHOP OF BATH AND WELLS
AND ARCHBISHOP OF BRISBANE

OXFORD UNIVERSITY PRESS
London   New York   Toronto

22 7 u
W181
1950

120179

Oxford University Press, Amen House, London E.C.4

GLASGOW NEW YORK TORONTO MELBOURNE WELLINGTON
BOMBAY CALCUTTA MADRAS CAPE TOWN

Geoffrey Cumberlege, Publisher to the University

PUBLISHED IN AUSTRALIA 1944
FIRST PUBLISHED IN ENGLAND 1946
SECOND IMPRESSION   1947
THIRD IMPRESSION   1950

*Printed in Great Britain
by Jarrold & Sons Ltd., Norwich*

Contents and Chronology

CONTENTS AND CHRONOLOGY

Introduction

THE decay of the habit of Bible reading is widely deplored: this volume is a humble effort to restore it. But not after the old fashion.

In the Victorian period the almost universal custom among pious people was to read a 'daily portion' or a chapter at a time. It was often read without much understanding, and the reader who, like the cook in Dickens, performed such devotions on retiring to rest, might sigh with appreciation if the chapter were not too long. Nevertheless the mere contact with Holy Writ was expected to exercise a good influence on the character. Probably it did, but not enough to enable the custom to maintain itself in a more prosaic and ruthless generation.

The present is an effort to encourage a different kind of Bible-reading, which will lead, not perhaps to close familiarity with favourite passages, but to knowledge of whole books. We need to grasp complete arguments, doctrines, schemes of salvation, not merely choice aphorisms or comforting texts. For this purpose we should read whole books of the Bible at a sitting, as we would read magazine articles or private communications.

If I sit down with a novel, I don't read one paragraph and then put it away. If I receive a letter from a friend, I don't read it a page at a time. It would be almost impossible to get the thread of either novel or letter that way; and it would certainly not be fair to the writer. It is a general rule in reading books that if we wish to understand what an author is trying to convey, we should read his production either as a whole or in the largest portions we have opportunity to assimilate.

Such a method applied to Scripture will be advantageous both to the general reader and to the student. The former usually knows the Bible only in snippets, and although isolated texts may mean a great deal to him, he could hardly tell you what any one of the prophets, or even S. Paul, preaches as his main theme.

Similarly, the young student who is often immersed in exegetical details, fails to see the wood for the trees.

In this publication I have had both types of reader in view, and have tried to produce something that can be read so quickly and easily that the main purpose of each document can be readily grasped.

The Epistles have been chosen for this experiment, because of all the New Testament writings they seem most to need this method of approach. The simplest readers can, without too much difficulty, understand the Gospels and Acts: the most learned cannot, without some special training in Jewish literature, understand the Revelation of S. John. But the Epistles occupy intermediate ground, where success depends largely upon one's own common sense. Actually, they are made more difficult than they need be when read in the official English versions. For older readers the language, whether Authorized or Revised, fails to 'bite' because it is already so familiar, while the young are repelled by its archaisms. For both it bears a specially refined and sacred aura not easily penetrable by the ordinary reader's intelligence, nourished mostly, as it is, on the English of the cheaper newspapers.

As for the more recent versions in modern English, valuable as they are (and I regard them as very valuable), they fail to meet the needs I have outlined, because they strive after too literal an accuracy. The consequence is that they read like anything but a piece of English prose, and are apt to prove slightly repellent to any but the determined reader.

I have tried to put the Epistles into the kind of language a Bishop might use in writing a monthly letter for his diocesan magazine, which, provided one's style is neither too stiff nor too colloquial, should offer a medium very like that of the original. The steps by which the result was achieved are as follows. First each letter was translated fresh from the Greek. Then it was gone over again, with a view to putting it where necessary (and it was nearly always necessary) into less stereotyped phraseology. During this latter process one did not shrink here and there from inserting an explanatory phrase or occasionally even a sentence. The result may be called either a free translation or a close paraphrase. But as the aim is to reproduce the argument of each writer in a readable form rather than to repeat his phrases with verbal accuracy, perhaps 'paraphrase' is the better term.

No one would claim that even when thus treated the longer epistles are altogether easy. S. Paul in particular is dealing with deep matters; the background of his thought is widely different from our own; and some of his illustrations are drawn from sources no longer familiar to us. But I shall have failed in my effort if S. Paul and his colleagues do not stand out from their own pages more human figures, and if their devotion to their Master and their highly individual presentations of His doctrine do not take on a clearer outline both for the general reader and for the young student.

At the Renaissance, when books were scarce and costly, people of all classes rushed to the churches to hear these letters read as soon as they had been translated into the English tongue. Now that books are cheap and plentiful, we ought to be at least as anxious to read them in our own homes. However, I feel sure that not until the early and heroic writers of the Christian Church have been made to speak in the language of our own time will they be spontaneously and eagerly read by our people.

WM. BRISBANE

BISHOPSBOURNE
BRISBANE
29 May 1943

THIS book was first published in Australia. The preparation of a new edition for this country has made possible the correction of textual errors and the re-writing of some of the verse translations. The book has also enjoyed the benefit of criticism by the Publishers' Reader, for which I am very grateful.

WM: LONDIN:

FULHAM PALACE, S.W.6

NOTE : *Chapters are shown in* Roman *and verses in* Arabic *numeral respectively.*

I and II Thessalonians

During his Second Missionary Journey S. Paul converted at Thessalonica (*the modern Salonica*) a mixed body of Jews and Pagans. Among the latter were many already converted to Judaism. But then, with his helper Silas, he was compelled to flee because of a protest violently lodged against him by the unconverted section of the Jews. (*Acts xvii.*)

Towards the end of this Journey Paul sent Timothy to visit the Thessalonian church while he himself was at work in Corinth. Timothy brought back a report which caused great relief mingled with a little anxiety. While the Christians had shewn commendable strength and courage under opposition, they had become unsettled about certain questions arising out of the expectation of Jesus' return in glory. Like most Christians of the period, they expected that return at any moment, and they were troubled about certain of their friends who, in the meantime, had reached, or might reach, the end of their mortal life. When the Lord returned to this earth, what part in His reign would be taken by those believers who had already died before He came?

The first of these two letters was written primarily to answer that question. At the same time S. Paul takes the opportunity to warn his readers of certain moral dangers threatening them and to defend his own reputation against aspersions cast upon it by unbelieving Jews.

The letter was perhaps too successful in its main purpose. While it eased the Thessalonians' anxiety about their departed friends, it gave some of them an exaggerated confidence in the immediacy of Christ's Second Coming. The Apostle therefore wrote the second letter to correct this impression, and to warn the Christians that they must not anticipate the end of the world by abandoning their ordinary pursuits. Happily, he was also able to congratulate them upon fresh reports of the fine example they were giving in Christian living.

First Letter To The Thessalonians

I

Paul, Silas and Timothy send greetings to the Church of Thessalonica in God the Father and our Lord Jesus Christ. Grace and peace be with you.

Thanks for their conversion

[2] When we mention you at our time of prayer, it is always with a special note of thanksgiving to God for you all, for we can never forget your loyal efforts, and your loving toil, and your persevering confidence in the coming of Our Lord Jesus Christ in the sight of God our Father. We recognize, brothers, how dear you are to God and what special favour He has shown you in singling you out to share in His redemption. This was evidenced by the fact that the Gospel we preached to you was not treated as mere words, but resulted in a great display of the Holy Spirit's power and of full conviction on your part. And this was possible in proportion as you refused to believe the slander about us, and accepted us for the men we really were among you and on your behalf.

[6] You followed no less an example than that of the Lord Himself in that, although acceptance of the Gospel involved much affliction, you did accept it with real spiritual joy. So you in your turn became examples to every one of the believers in Macedonia and Achaia. Starting from you, not only has the word of the Lord resounded in Macedonia and Achaia, but the report of your loyalty towards God has spread everywhere. Indeed there has really been no need for us to say anything, for the reports themselves describe the result of our visit to you. They tell how you turned from idols to serve the true and living God, and how you are now joined with us in awaiting the return from

heaven of His Son, whom He raised from the dead, that is to say
Jesus, our rescuer from the wrath to come.

II

Reminder of the first visit

Of course, you remember yourselves, my brothers, the circumstances of our first visit. It was no ineffective meeting. As you
know, we had been ill-treated and insulted at Philippi. Yet in
spite of the opposition we were inspired with a supernatural
courage to tell you about the Gospel of God. Our appeal does
not spring from illusion or from impure motives, nor is it based
on deceit. But we speak only as our loyalty to the Gospel has
been tried and tested by God, and we do it in order to please not
men but God, who is indeed the Assayer of our motives. We
never had recourse to flattery, as you know; nor did we ever
seek a plausible excuse to fill our pockets at your expense. God
is our witness to that. Nor did we look for honours at the hands
of men, either yourselves or others—though we might have de-
manded something more than respect as Christ's Apostles. On
the contrary we behaved among you with great gentleness, like
a nursing mother ministering to her children. Such was our
yearning over you that we would gladly have shared with you
not only the Gospel of God but our very lives—so dear had you
become to us.

[9] May I remind you, brothers, that we actually supported
ourselves by manual labour. We worked at our trade day and
night in order that while we preached to you the Gospel of God
we should not be a burden to any of you. You know very well,
as God also does, how pious and upright and irreproachable was
our behaviour among the faithful. Similarly, you know how we
urged you, just like a father his children, both by precept and
example to conduct yourselves worthily of the God Who has
invited you to enter His Kingdom and His glory.

[13] We have a special reason for giving God continual thanks,
namely that, when you received the word of Divine revelation
from our lips you welcomed it, not as a merely human message,

but for what it really is, a message from God. And indeed it does work with effect in you who believe. You, my brothers, have followed in the footsteps of the churches of God in Judæa which accepted Christianity: you have experienced the same suffering at the hands of your fellow-countrymen as they did at the hands of the Jews. Those same Jews, not content with having killed the Lord Jesus and the prophets, and with having persecuted us, now go on to put themselves out of favour with God and in opposition to everyone else by setting obstacles in the way of our preaching to the Pagans with a view to their salvation. It seems as if at every moment of their history they must be filling up the measure of their sins. They will find that Divine Wrath is awaiting them at the end.

Anxiety about the Thessalonians' Welfare

[17] We, brethren, have felt like orphans bereft during the short season we have been separated from you. 'Out of sight' did not mean 'out of mind'; and we have longed all the more ardently for the moment when we should catch sight of you again. For that reason alone we intended to pay you a visit—I certainly did myself, more than once—but Satan put an obstacle in the way. For who will be our hope and joy and crowning pride in the presence of our Lord Jesus on the day of His appearing? Who, indeed, except yourselves? You are our glory and our joy.

III

That's how it happened that when I could bear it no longer I decided to carry on alone in Athens, and sent Timothy, our brother and God's minister in the Gospel of Christ, to strengthen you and comfort you in respect of your faith, so that no one should be wheedled away from it in the midst of these troubles. You know well enough that we are born to trouble; and when I was with you I warned you that there would be trouble; and now, as you see, it has turned out true.

[5] So when I could no longer bear the suspense, I sent to inquire about your loyalty for fear that the Tempter had tempted you and our labour had been in vain. But now that Timothy has

returned and has brought us the good news of your loyalty and love, and that you always have kindly thoughts of me, longing to see me just as I long to see you—why, for all this I am greatly cheered, brethren, because of your loyalty in the midst of all my distress and trouble. I really feel alive again, now that I know you are holding your ground in the Lord. How can I thank God sufficiently for all the joy you have caused me to feel before Him. Day and night I pray with insistence that I may be allowed to see you again and put right any deficiencies there may be in your faith. May God Himself, our Father and our Lord Jesus, make clear for me a way to visit you. And as for you, I hope that the Lord will make your love to each other, and indeed to all men, increase to overflowing; just as ours does to you, so that when our Lord Jesus appears with all His saints you may be established in the presence of our God and Father with your conscience free from any blame in respect of holiness.

IV

Exhortation to Purity, Love and Work

For the rest, brethren, we entreat you and call upon you in the Lord Jesus to put into practice the lessons we have taught you. You have learnt from us what kind of conduct you must practise in order to please God; and you behave accordingly. Well, continue to do so to the full extent of your ability. You know what words of command we passed on to you with the authority of the Lord Jesus. 'God's will for you is complete sanctification.' You must abstain from all sexual impurity; each of you must know how to maintain his relations with his wife on a level of reverent chastity, not of lustful possession like the Pagans who are ignorant of God. And no one must stoop to outwit or overreach a brother in a matter of this kind, for the Lord Himself sees justice done in all such cases—but of that He gave you due and solemn warning. God did not call us to live a life of impurity, but to perfect our sanctification. He who deliberately ignores this fact puts a slight not on any human teacher, but on God, who actually bestows upon us His own Spirit, the very Spirit of sanctification.

[9]   There is no need for me to write anything to you about the special love we ought to show towards our brethren of the Christian Church. On your own account you have accepted the Divine teaching that we must love one another. And indeed you have gone so far in carrying it out as to take all the brethren in the whole of Macedonia within your scope. I only ask you now to give the principle still fuller application. Let your ambition be to live a quiet life without interfering with other people's business, but working for yourselves at some handicraft—as I have already instructed you. That would ensure that your conduct would appear correct in the eyes of non-Christians and would prevent any necessity for sponging on one another.

Problems concerning the Departed

[13]   I do not wish you to be left in ignorance, brethren, about the condition of the Christians who die before the Lord's final coming. You must not grieve for your dead as those do who have no hope of a final reunion. If we believe that Jesus died and rose again, we must also believe that (since Jesus and His members are inseparable) God will cause those who have fallen asleep in Him to return with Him. This I affirm on the Lord's own authority: that we who are still alive at His coming will have no advantage in point of time over those already dead. This is how it will happen. At the appointed summons, given by the voice of the Archangel and the trumpet call of God, the Lord will descend from Heaven in person. The Christian dead will rise first. Then, and not till then, shall we who are still alive be caught up together with them in the clouds and meet the Lord in the air. So shall we be always with the Lord.

[18]   From these considerations you can derive comfort and encouragement for one another.

V

Concerning the Second Advent

There is no need for me to say anything about the date and circumstances of the Lord's coming. You have been carefully instructed that the Day of the Lord approaches like a thief in the night. Just when people are announcing Peace and Safety, at that moment will destruction come upon them unawares, as inevitably as birth-pangs upon a pregnant woman. There is no escape.

[4] But you, brethren, are not in such spiritual darkness that the Day will overtake you like a thief. You are all children of the light and of the day: we do not belong to night and darkness. Therefore we must not be drunk with sleep like those others, but we must be watchful and sober. Night is the time when the drowsy sleep and the drunkards fuddle themselves. But we who belong to the day keep sober. Like soldiers on the watch, we have put on the breast-plate of faith and love, and as a helmet our hope of salvation. God has not marked us out for wrath, but for the accomplishment of salvation through our Lord Jesus Christ, who has died for us, in order that, sleeping or waking, we may live in His company. So encourage one another, and each build up the other—as indeed you already do.

Exhortation to Discipline

[12] I hope, brethren, you will recognize the authority of those workers among you who are in positions of leadership and instruction. Hold them in special affection for the work they do. Live at peace with one another. I especially ask you, brothers, to discipline the unruly, to encourage the faint-hearted, to strengthen the weak, to show patience towards all. See that you do not return evil for evil, but try always to bring about the greatest good for each other and for everyone. Cultivate a happy disposition. Pray continually; and in all circumstances give thanks, for that is God's will for you in Christ Jesus. Do not stifle the gift of the Spirit, or disregard His leadings through prophecy. Put them all to the test: hold fast to that which is good, but leave severely alone every sort of evil.

[23] May the God of Peace Himself make you completely sanctified. And may your body, soul and spirit be preserved entirely without reproach against the coming of our Lord Jesus

2

Christ. He who called you is reliable and will accomplish what He promised.

[25] Brethren, pray for us. Convey my salutation to all the brethren with the sacred kiss. I charge you by the Lord to have this letter read to all the brethren.

The grace of our Lord Jesus Christ be with you.

S. Paul's Second Letter
To The Thessalonians

I

Paul, Silas and Timothy send greetings to the Church of
Thessalonica. We recall our common bond with you in God our
Father and in our Lord Jesus Christ; and we pray that they will
grant you the blessings of grace and peace.

Thanksgiving

[3] We feel, brothers, that we owe God a debt of eternal gratitude. Certainly we ought to be continually thanking Him for
the immense loyalty you have shown and for the mutual love
which increasingly animates each one of you. That is why we
have been able with pride to draw the attention of all the churches
of God to the fortitude and faith you have shown in all the
persecutions and afflictions you have endured. One day that
will be evidence before the Judgment Seat of God that you have
proved yourselves worthy of the Kingdom of God, the Kingdom
on behalf of which you are now called upon to endure suffering.
Then God's justice will repay those who now afflict you by sending affliction upon them, and by granting to you who are now
afflicted the privilege of sharing with us a complete rest from
affliction.

[7] That will happen when our Lord Jesus Christ is revealed
from Heaven in the midst of flaming fire surrounded by the
angels who are ministers of His power. Then He will inflict
punishment on those who ignore God and refuse to obey the
gospel of our Lord Jesus Christ. They will suffer the penalty of
eternal destruction and of banishment from the presence of the
Lord and from the glory of His strength, when He comes on that
great day to be glorified by His saints and to awake the wonder

of all believers.   Among these last we know that you will be
numbered, because you believed our teaching.

[11]   We always pray for you, asking that God may make you
worthy of His calling and that He may bring all His kindly good-
will and work of faith to so powerful a degree of perfection in
you that by you the glorious reputation of our Lord Jesus Christ
may be still further enhanced.   Similarly, we pray that your
glory may be enhanced by Him in accordance with the gracious
favour shown us by our God and the Lord Jesus Christ.

II

Misapprehensions about the Second Coming

In connection, brothers, with the coming of our Lord Jesus
Christ and our summons to attend Him, we ask you not to be
easily upset or troubled in your mind. No matter what pretended
revelation people may point to or what argument they may use,
or even what forged letter they may produce as if it came from
us, there is no need to believe that the Day of the Lord is already
upon us. Do not let anybody deceive you in any way. There
must be certain premonitory signs, such as the great apostasy,
and the revelation of the Lawless One, the Destroyer, the
Antagonist, who will exalt himself against everything that is
reckoned Divine or sacred, setting himself against the Holy Place
and claiming Divinity for himself.

[5]   Don't you remember that when I was staying with you I
used to tell you about all this? And now you can recognize the
Restraining Power that holds the Antagonist in check, so that he
can only be revealed in his appointed time. For the mysterious
principle of lawlessness is already set to do its fell work, but it
cannot be fully manifested until the Restraining Power, which is
also there, has been taken away.

[8]   Then the Lawless One will be fully revealed. But the Lord
Jesus will destroy him by merely breathing upon him and will
reduce him to impotence by the mere manifestation of His
presence. This appearance of the Lawless One is in accord with
the machinations of Satan. He is already hard at work with

lying signs and portents and with every sort of device to deceive those who are even now perishing as a result of their refusal to accept the True Love that would save them. Such misguided people God afflicts with a preference for error, so that they believe what is false. Thus all those who refuse to believe the truth and prefer evil will be ripe for judgment.

Exhortation to stand fast

[13] But we certainly ought to be thanking God continually on your account, beloved brethren, because He has chosen you from all eternity to enjoy the blessings of salvation through the sanctifying influence of the Holy Spirit and through loyal acceptance of the truth. To this end He called you by the instrumentality of my preaching of the Gospel to make you sure of ultimately sharing the glory of our Lord Jesus Christ. Therefore, my brethren, stand fast and keep tight hold of the traditions which you have been taught both by word of mouth and by our letter. May our Lord Jesus Christ Himself and God our Father, who has loved you and given you unbounded comfort and encouragement and a good hope in grace, grant you calmness of heart and strength to perform every kind deed and word.

III

Warning against disorderly conduct

For the rest, brethren, do not fail to remember us in your prayers, and ask that the Lord's word may enjoy elsewhere the same swift and glorious acceptance as it did in your case. Pray, too, that we may be delivered from outrageous and wicked men, for there are some who are rank unbelievers. You can rely upon the Lord, who will strengthen you and protect you from the Evil One. It is on Him that we base our confidence with regard to you, that you are not only doing, but will continue to do, the things we enjoin. May He direct your hearts to imitate God's own love and Christ's hopeful endurance of opposition.

[6] Brothers, in the name of the Lord Jesus Christ we bid you separate yourselves from every brother whose conduct is dis-

orderly and out of accord with the tradition you received from us. You know that we ourselves gave you a good example to follow, for there was no ambiguity about the way we behaved when we stayed with you. We would not even let anyone entertain us without payment. We spent days and nights in laborious toil so that we should not be a burden to you. As a matter of fact, we had a perfect right to ask for hospitality, but we wanted to provide a good example for you to imitate. And indeed when we were with you we laid special emphasis on the fact that if anyone was unwilling to work he ought not to be given his food.

[11]   Reports are reaching us that there are some of you who are leading ill-regulated lives, trifling away their time instead of working. To them we send instructions, and indeed our positive command in the Lord Jesus Christ, that they set themselves to work without distraction and earn their own living. But to the rest of you we say, 'Do not deviate from the excellent course of conduct you have already adopted.' If anyone refuses to obey the instructions we have given in this letter, let him be a marked man; refrain from all intercourse with him; and so make him hang his head in shame. You need not treat him as an enemy, but direct him as a brother. In whatever state of commotion you may be from time to time may the Lord of peace Himself grant you continued and abiding peace. The Lord be with you all.

I, Paul, add the concluding salutation in my own hand. That is the assurance of genuineness in every letter we send. You can tell the writing. Here it is: *The Grace of our Lord Jesus Christ be with you all.*

Galatians

The address of this letter is probably intended to cover those churches of Southern Galatia, such as Iconium, Lystra and Derbe, which S. Paul had founded on his First Missionary Journey and visited on his Second. The time of its dispatch was soon after he had reached Syrian Antioch at the end of his Second Journey.

The reason for its composition was as follows: Paul had heard that agents of the Jewish Christian party were insisting that his Galatian converts should be circumcised and keep the other regulations of the Mosaic Law. To him this seemed a complete contradiction of the free grace of the Gospel and a denial of the sufficiency of the redemption gained by Christ. He was willing that converts from among the Jews should continue to keep their old national customs if they wished, but they must not try to impose them on converts from other nations. Such observances were in no sense necessary for salvation.

With the clarity of genius, S. Paul had long seen that if the 'Judaisers' had their way they would make of the Christian Church a mere esoteric circle within Judaism instead of the universal Divine Society intended by its Founder. That issue had been thrashed out and decided in the council held at Jerusalem and described for us in Acts xv. With great eloquence and spiritual force the Apostle here shows why he intends to hold the whole Church to the decision then reached.

A Letter To The Churches Of Galatia

From Paul,

who has been appointed an Apostle—not by any man or to represent any body of men, but by Jesus Christ and by God the Father who raised Him from the dead,

to the churches of Galatia.

Greetings

[2] Our people here join with me in sending greetings. May grace and peace be yours from God our Father and our Lord Jesus Christ. Jesus gave Himself for our sins in order that He might rescue us from this present evil world, and by so doing carry out the will of our God and Father, whose is the glory for ever and ever. Amen.

Reproaches

[6] I am amazed at the rapidity with which you are turning away from the Apostles, who converted you to the grace of Christ, in order to follow some quite different gospel, which is actually no gospel at all. Obviously, there is someone who is creating confusion in your minds and is determined to revolutionize the gospel of Christ. But if ever I myself or an angel from Heaven preach to you any other gospel than the one I actually did preach, then let God's curse fall upon us. I repeat that : if anyone preach to you any other form of the Gospel than the one you have already received, God's curse be on him.

The Origin of Paul's teaching

[10] Who is the umpire in this debate, God or man? Am I to try to tickle *men's* ears? If up till now I have been merely trying

to satisfy men, I should be no servant of Christ. I would have you know, brothers, that the Gospel I preach is no product of human invention. I did not receive it from any man, nor was I ever taught it. It was revealed to me by Jesus Christ.

[13] You have heard of my reputation in the service of Judaism, how relentlessly I persecuted the Church of God and ravaged it. You know that I was conspicuous among my fellow countrymen and contemporaries for my extreme zeal on behalf of our national customs. But when God (who had indeed set me apart from my birth and favoured me with His special call), was pleased to reveal His Son to me in order that I might preach Him among the Pagans, I immediately cut myself off from all human contacts. I did not even go up to Jerusalem to confer with those who were His apostolic delegates before me, but I first went away to Arabia and afterwards came back to Damascus. It was not until three years after that I went up to Jerusalem to interview Cephas, and stayed with him a fortnight. I did not see any of the other Apostles except James, the Lord's brother. (I assure you that in giving these details I am telling you the exact truth.) I then went to the districts of Syria and Cilicia. To the Jewish synagogues that had come over to Christianity I was not even known by sight. All they were told was, 'Our former persecutor is now a preacher of the faith he once tried to destroy.' And that made them give God thanks because of me.

II

The Circumcision Question

It was only after an interval of fourteen years that I again went up to Jerusalem in company with Barnabas and Titus. (That journey I undertook in response to a revelation.) I then set before them the Gospel as I preach it to the Pagans—but only privately before the leaders. I did not want to have all my past and present trouble in vain. Although my companion, Titus, was a Greek, no compulsion was then exercised upon him to be circumcised.

[4]   However, as the result of the intervention of certain so-called 'brothers', who were dragged in to spy upon the liberty we enjoyed in Christ Jesus so as to enslave us again, questions were raised. But not for one moment did we submit to the dictation of those interlopers. We were determined at all costs to uphold the true Gospel for your sakes.

[6]   But from those who were apparently the leaders—what they were doesn't matter, office and position count for nothing with God—from them I received no fresh information. On the contrary, realizing that I had been entrusted with the mission to the non-Jews as Peter with that to the Jews, and recognizing the grace given me, James, Peter and John, who were reckoned as the principals, extended the right hand of fellowship both to myself and to Barnabas, so that we might continue to address ourselves to the Pagans, as they to the Jews.

All they asked us to do was to remember the poor, which, of course, I was very anxious to do.

[11]   But when Cephas came to Antioch I found myself in violent opposition to him, because he was obviously at fault.   Until certain emissaries arrived from James, he made no difficulty about sharing meals with non-Jewish Christians. But when they came he cut himself off from the Gentile section of our society because he was afraid of those who insisted that everybody should be circumcised. The rest of our Jewish members followed his example, so that even Barnabas became involved in their defection.

[14]   When I saw that they were not keeping straight by the truth of the Gospel, I said to Cephas in front of them all, 'If you who are a Jew can conform with the customs of the Pagans and not follow your own, how can you compel Pagans to accept Jewish customs as necessary?' Even we, although we were born Jews and not Pagan outlaws, know that a man is not reckoned righteous through keeping the Law, but only through faith in Christ Jesus. And we ourselves put our trust in Christ Jesus in order that we might be reckoned righteous through faith in Christ and not through deeds done in obedience to the Law. For

no human being can obtain acquittal by mere observance of the Law.

[17]   But, you may object, if, as sinners trying to get ourselves acquitted, we take refuge with Christ, does not that make Him a partner in our sins?   Certainly not.   On the other hand, if I begin to reconstruct the false defence I have already destroyed, I certainly convict myself as a transgressor.   For once, as a result of the Law's action, I died to the Law in order that I might live to God.   I have been actually crucified with Christ.   Consequently the 'I' that is now living is no longer myself, but Christ who lives in me.   The essence of the life that I now live in this world is loyalty to the Son of God who loved me and gave Himself for me. I do not churlishly refuse the free gift of God—for obviously if you try to earn righteousness by the Law you prove Christ's death to have been in vain.

III

Faith, not Law, the means of Salvation

You poor, foolish Galatians, by whom have you let yourselves be bewitched—you, before whose eyes the crucified Christ has been so vividly portrayed?   There is just one question I would like to ask you—the gift of the Spirit, did you get that by keeping the Law or by accepting the Gospel?   How can you be so silly? Having made a start in the sphere of Spirit, do you now want to gain your ends by switching over to the sphere of Matter?   Have you had such an experience for nothing?   Yes, I suppose it may have been for nothing.   But really, when God gives you the Spirit and works miracles among you, does He do it by means of your obedience to the Law or through your acceptance of the Gospel? You know what is said about Abraham, 'He believed in God, and that simple acceptance was accredited to him as righteousness.'

[7]   Understand now that the real sons of Abraham are all those who place their reliance on faith.   The Scripture, foreseeing that God would one day acquit the Pagans on the ground of faith, makes to Abraham an anticipatory announcement of the Gospel,

'You shall become a blessing to all the heathen.' So all those who rely on faith are blessed along with faithful Abraham. On the other hand, all those who rely on their ability to carry out the Law are subject to a curse. For it is written, 'Cursed are all those who do not abide by every article in the Law and carry it out.' However, it is clear that no one can win acquittal before God by keeping the Law, for it says, 'The just man shall live by his faith.' Whereas the Law does not demand faith, but action: 'He who does certain things shall live by them.'

[13] Now, Christ bought us off the curse of the Law at the cost of being accursed for our sakes, as it says, 'Cursed is everyone who suffers a criminal's death.' That is how Abraham's blessing may be extended to non-Jews through Christ Jesus: we may receive the promised Spirit through faith. Take a simple analogy: an ordinary contract, such as a will, when it has been signed cannot be set aside or altered. That is what happened when promises were made to Abraham and to his 'descendant'. It does not say 'descendants' in the plural, but in the singular, 'to his descendant', and that, of course, means Christ. So I repeat, the contract with Abraham, which was already confirmed by God, cannot be superseded by the Law, which did not come into existence till four centuries later. The Law did not cancel God's promise.

[18] Of course if our inheritance is legally entailed, then there is no need of a specially contracted promise. But in Abraham's case God did promise it as a free gift. Where, then, did the Law come in? It was added to the scheme in order to correct man's sin, until the 'descendant' should appear for whom the promise was made. And it was conveyed by angels through an intermediary, Moses. (It is obvious that an intermediary acts for more than one party; in this case the other is God.)

[21] Is the Law then in conflict with the promises of God? By no means. If a Law could have been produced which would have guaranteed life, then righteousness would have come by the Law. But the Scriptures have regarded the whole universe as implicated in sin in order that the blessing promised to faith in Jesus Christ might be enjoyed by all believers without difference or distinction.

[23] Before the era of faith began we were guarded by the Law, constrained to wait until Faith was revealed. The Law was like that domestic slave whose duty it is to conduct children safely to school. So the Law brought us to Christ in order that we might be put right by Faith. When Faith came we no longer needed the slave to keep us under surveillance. Now you are all sons of God through faith in Christ Jesus, for all who have been baptized into Christ have clothed themselves with His life and character. In that condition there is no longer any distinction between Jew and Greek, between slave and free, between male and female. You are all one in Christ Jesus. If you belong to Christ, you are the true descendants of Abraham and his proper heirs, not by legal descent, but in virtue of the Promise.

IV

What it means to be a Son

All the same the heir, during his minority, is little better than a slave, although he is destined to be master of all. He is put under guardians and tutors until the time appointed by his father. So we, while we were in our spiritual childhood, were under the control of elemental forces. But when the right moment arrived, God sent His Son, born by means of a human birth and consequently subject to the Law, to redeem those who were subject to the Law, in order that we might be made His sons by adoption. And once you became His sons God sent the Spirit of His Son into your hearts to give expression to the fact of your sonship by addressing Him as 'Our Father'. So then you are no longer servants but sons, and if sons then also heirs—so constituted by God Himself.

[8] Formerly in your ignorance of the true God you rendered a slavish service to those who in reality were no gods. But now that you have recognized God, or rather have been recognized by Him, how can you turn back to those weak and beggarly Elements and make up your mind to serve them again? Already you are busy with special observances of days and months and seasons and years. I am beginning to be afraid for you, that somehow I have toiled over you in vain.

[12] Brothers, I urge you, do as I do; for after all I am one of yourselves. I am not complaining that you have done me any harm. You remember that it was owing to a bout of sickness that I was first put in a position to preach the Gospel to you. You did not turn your backs upon me or despise me because of the distressing nature of that experience, but you gave me the kind of welcome you might have given to an angel of God, or to Christ Himself. What has happened to that spontaneous cordiality of yours? I am sure that then, if it had been possible, you would have plucked out your very eyes and given them to me. Have I become your enemy because I tell you the truth? There are others who cultivate your friendship now, but to no good purpose. They want to isolate you, so that you will be forced to cultivate them. Well, it is nice for you to be sought after all the time, and not only when I am with you. My dear children, I feel as if I were suffering birth-pangs all over again for you, waiting for Christ to be formed in you. I wish I could be with you at this moment and put more eloquence into my plea. I am really at a loss what to do about you.

[21] Tell me, you who want to be under the Law, don't you take any notice of the Law? Well, listen to this. It is written, 'Abraham had two sons, one born of a slave, the other of a free woman. The child of the slave was born in the ordinary course of nature, but the child of the free woman was born in fulfilment of a divine promise.' Now that is a picture of our spiritual state. The two women correspond to two agreements, the one made on Mt. Sinai when the Law was given. That involves us all in slavery, as is implied in the slave-wife Hagar who corresponds to Mt. Sinai in Arabia, the place where the Law was given. And that mountain stands also for the present city of Jerusalem, which with all its inhabitants is a slave to the Law. But our mother is a free woman, the New Jerusalem from heaven.

> The empty house resounds with joy,
>   The childless wife breaks into song;
> To her who was bereft of all,
>   Unnumbered children now belong.

And you, my brothers, are what Isaac was—the children of a promise. But as in his case the son who was born in the natural way bullied the one who was born after a spiritual fashion, so it is now. Nevertheless, what does the Scripture say? 'Repudiate the slave-woman and her son. The slave's son cannot share the inheritance with the son born in freedom.'

Well, brothers, we are not children of the slave-woman, but of the free.

V

What Freedom means

Christ has made us completely, utterly free. Stand firm then, and do not let yourselves slip back under any yoke of servitude. I, Paul, assure you most solemnly that if you let yourselves be circumcised you will forfeit all the advantage you have from your Christianity. I affirm again to every man who has let himself be circumcised that he has become responsible for keeping the whole Law.

[4] If you try to put yourselves right with God by obeying the Law you cut yourselves off from Christ and drop right outside the sphere of grace. For we have been given a guarantee that we shall be made righteous, not by the Law, but by the Spirit through the operation of faith. If you are attached to Jesus Christ, it does not matter whether you are circumcised or not, the only thing of importance is the faith that works through love.

[7] You were getting along admirably: who was it interfered with your obedience to the truth? Such enticement certainly did not come from the one who called you. It is extraordinary how far an evil influence can spread. But I rely on you in the Lord not to let these wrong notions go any further. He who is unsettling you will have to face his punishment, whoever he is. In any case, it is obvious that I have not changed my teaching. If I were now preaching circumcision should I be undergoing persecution? In such case the 'scandal' of the cross would indeed be neutralized. Why don't those who upset you about circumcision get themselves castrated completely, and done with it!

[13] It is clear then, brothers, that you were called to be free. Only don't go to extremes and make your freedom an excuse for licence, but give yourselves to the service of each other in love. For the whole Law is summed up in the one sentence, 'Thou shalt love thy neighbour as thyself.' On the other hand if you snap at one another and get your teeth into one another, you will have to be singularly careful to avoid destroying one another. What I mean to say is, let your conduct be guided by the Spirit and you will cease to pursue merely selfish interests. Our lower self is always at war with the spirit and the spirit with the self, for they are complete opposites. The result is that you cannot attain your ideal. However, if you follow the lead of the Spirit, you are at least untrammelled by the Law.

[19] The characteristic traits of our lower nature are quite easy to distinguish, as follows: immorality, impurity, sensuality, idolatry, magic, quarrels, strife, envy, jealousy, anger, rivalry, factions, false teaching, envy, drunkenness, debauchery and all that kind of thing. I warn you about this again, as I have done before, that those who are guilty of such practices shall not inherit the Kingdom of God. But the characteristic expression of the Spirit is love, joy, peace, patience, kindness, goodness, faith, gentleness, self-control. Against such things there is no Law. Those who belong to Jesus Christ have crucified the lower nature with its passions and lusts. If, then, the Spirit is the source of our life, let Him be the guide of our conduct. Let us not put on bombastic airs or show ourselves provoking and jealous towards one another.

VI

Practical Hints

Brothers, if a man is caught out in any kind of fault, let those of you who are 'spiritual' put him right, but gently and considerately, keeping an eye on yourselves in case you too are tempted. Bear one another's burdens and so fulfil the Law of Christ. If a man begins to think a good deal of himself, he is suffering from self-deception, for he is really nothing. Let each man learn to criticize his own work, then only can he be satisfied with self-commendation and have no need to look for flattery from others. Each man must bear his own share of responsibility.

[6]   A man who is under instruction should see that his teacher is properly recompensed. You must not be niggardly. Do not make any mistake; we cannot deceive God; we reap precisely what we sow. If we sow seeds appropriate to our lower nature, we shall from that very nature reap corruption; but if we sow seed appropriate to the Spirit, we shall from the Spirit reap eternal life. And do not tire of your good efforts; in due time we shall have our harvest if we persevere. So, as we have opportunity, let us serve the interests of others, especially of those who belong to the faithful circle of Christians.

P.S.

[11]   Here is a postscript in my own handwriting. (You can tell it is mine by the big letters I make.) Those people who insist on you being circumcised are trying to make as big a show as they can, and they hope that by so doing they will avoid being persecuted for professing to believe in the cross of Christ. They who are circumcised fail to keep the Law themselves and yet they want to get you circumcised just in order to boast of your submission to a purely formal ceremony. As far as I am concerned, the only thing I should ever want to boast about is precisely that cross of our Lord Jesus Christ, on which the world has been crucified to me and I to the world. The fact is that neither circumcision nor uncircumcision counts for anything. The one thing of importance is that we should be created afresh in a new order of existence.

[16]   May peace and mercy rest upon all those who acknowledge this fundamental requirement. That means God's New Israel. After this let no man worry me any further, for the scars *my* body bears are those of the Lord Jesus. Brothers, the grace of our Lord Jesus Christ be with you. Amen.

I and II Corinthians

S. Paul appears to have written four letters to the church of Corinth. While I Corinthians is a distinct unit, II Corinthians contains the whole or parts of three letters. These are, in the order of their composition, vi. 14–vii. 1, x.–xiii., and i.–ix. (omitting vi. 14–vii. 1). The following is the historical setting in which they were written.

During his Second Missionary Journey Paul visited Corinth, a cosmopolitan port renowned for its culture and notorious for its immorality. There he converted a very mixed body of Jews, Roman colonists and native Greeks. The unconverted section of the Jews tried to make trouble for him, but the Roman Governor, Gallio, refused to interfere. After Paul's departure, however, other troubles arose within the Christian community owing to the loose and turbulent character of the citizens, in which even the converts seem to have shared.

a. When S. Paul was in Ephesus at the start of his Third Missionary Journey he heard news from Corinth which made it necessary for him to write and warn his people against associating with immoral persons. The essential part of this letter is probably to be found in II Cor. vi. 14–vii. 1.

b. Soon afterwards he received an official letter from the church of Corinth asking for advice on certain matters, such as the correct method of celebrating the Lord's Supper and the doctrine of the resurrection. Also he heard, through some members of the household of Chloe, that party spirit was rife and that a particularly grave case of immorality had arisen in the church. With all these questions he dealt in the letter now known to us as I Corinthians. This he dispatched by the short sea route, and at the same time he sent Timothy by the longer land route to deal with the situation in person.

c. Neither the letter nor Timothy's influence had the desired effect; and so S. Paul proceeded to Corinth himself. However, even he was unable to effect a reform, and, after being grossly affronted, he left and returned to Ephesus. From there he wrote the 'severe' letter (his third), which is found in II Cor. x.–xiii. This was carried by Titus, who, as an older and more experienced man than Timothy, was expected to win *back the Corinthians to a proper regard for Christian morality and to a proper respect for their original leader.*

d. In the meantime, Paul continued his Third Missionary Journey. Somewhere in Macedonia he was met by Titus, who brought him the good news that the Corinthians were ready to conform, and that they had already by a majority vote censured the person who had been so rude to S. Paul. The Apostle immediately wrote his fourth letter (II Cor. i.–ix., omitting vi. 14–vii. 1), in which he forgives his traducer, closes the controversy, and arranges for a collection to be taken for the poverty-stricken Christians in Jerusalem.

In the following paraphrase the received order is retained, but the reader will gain a more intelligent view of the circumstances if he follows the sequence given above.

First Letter To The Christians
In Corinth

I

From Paul, divinely appointed Apostle of Jesus Christ, and Brother Sosthenes to the Church of God in Corinth, Greeting.

You have been made holy in Christ Jesus and called to be saints. I wish you, together with all those everywhere who call upon the name of Jesus Christ, the one Lord of us all, every grace and peace from God our Father and the Lord Jesus Christ.

Thanksgiving

[4] I always thank God in regard to you for the grace of God given you in Christ Jesus. In Him you have found abundant riches of every kind, especially such as are implied in advanced knowledge of the faith and arguments wherewith to defend it. In proportion as this is so my preaching about Christ has been confirmed in your own experience. So now you are not lacking in any gift, while you wait for the final revelation of our Lord Jesus Christ, who will confirm you to the very end, and will see that you are acquitted in the great Day of Judgment. You can always depend upon God, for it was He who called you to participate in the divine sonship of Jesus Christ our Lord.

Party Spirit

[10] I beseech you, brothers, in the name of our Lord Jesus Christ, to aim at unanimity and to avoid dissensions. Try to achieve a common mind and will. Chloe's people have reported to me, my brothers, that there are factions among you. By that I mean that you are divided into cliques. One of you says, 'I follow Paul'; and another, 'I follow Apollos'; and another, 'I follow Peter'; and another, 'I follow Christ.' Is then Christ divided? Was Paul crucified for you? Were you baptized in the

name of Paul? I am thankful that I baptized none of you except Crispus and Gaius. No one can say that you were baptized in my name. But yes, I also baptized the family of Stephanas. I don't think I baptized anyone else besides them. The duty Christ laid upon me was not that of baptizing, but of preaching. And even that I was not to do with any special learning or eloquence, for fear that the simple message of the cross might lose its effectiveness.

The Simplicity of the Cross

[18] The argument of the cross is mere stupidity to those who are on the way to perdition, but to us who tread the way of salvation it is the very power of God. In the Bible God says:

> The wisdom of the wise will I destroy,
> And all the sages' logic bring to naught.

What has happened to the sage and the scribe? What has become of the worldly critic? Has not God stultified worldly wisdom? When in the wisdom of God the world was allowed to fail in its effort to comprehend Him by the use of its own wisdom, He arranged for the salvation of believers through the 'stupidity' of plain and simple preaching. So while the Jews ask for a sign and the Greeks look for a philosophy, we preach Christ crucified, a stumbling-block to the Jews and stupidity to the Greeks, but to the elect Christ the power of God and the wisdom of God. God's 'stupid cross' reveals a greater wisdom than that of men, and His weakness a greater strength than theirs.

[26] Look at your own vocation, brethren. It does not include many philosophers, leading men, or folk of gentle birth; but God has chosen the simplicities of this world to confound the wise and its frailties to confound the strong; the mean and despised has He chosen, the things that are emptied of all existence, to overwhelm what is already in being. His aim is to prevent any mortal from having an excuse to boast before God. Of His free gift it comes that you are in Christ Jesus, who has become for us the wisdom of God, and holiness, righteousness and redemp-

tion. Thus the saying is proved true, 'Our only ground of assurance is in the Lord.'

II

Paul's Teaching

When I came among you, brethren, I did not come with any
obvious eloquence or intellectual ability to proclaim God's secret
purpose. I determined indeed to put aside all knowledge while
I was among you except that of Jesus Christ and the fact that He
was crucified on our behalf. While I was with you I was terribly
weak and nervous and timid. My speaking and preaching were
certainly not marked by any specially persuasive quality, but
solely by plain and forceful revelation of the Spirit. So you did
not learn to put your trust in human subtlety, but in the power
of God.

[6] I am ready to speak of 'wisdom' among the fully initiated,
but not the wisdom of this world nor of the demonic rulers of this
world, who are already in their decline. I speak the wisdom of
God enshrined in His secret purpose. God ordained it before this
world began in order to reveal its glory to us. Not one of the
rulers of this world has known it; if they had known it they would
not have crucified the Lord of glory. You remember the lines:

> What eye has not seen and ear has not heard,
>   And surpasses the desire of the heart,
> God alone has discerned and in secret prepared
>   For the joy of His lovers apart.

This revelation God has given us through His Spirit, for the
Spirit fathoms everything, even God's own deep designs. Just as
in the case of human beings no one can really understand what
is peculiar to an individual except his own inner spirit, so no one
understands what is peculiar to God except the Spirit of God.
Those are the subjects of which we treat in our addresses. We
deliver our sermons not in the terms of oratorical skill, but in
language taught by the Spirit, fitting a spiritual subject to a
spiritual manner of approach.

[14] The unregenerate man cannot grasp what comes from the Spirit of God; it is foolishness to him and he cannot understand it, because it is clear only to spiritual discernment. But the spiritually minded man has the right standpoint from which to appreciate everything, although he himself may not be appreciated by anybody. Who, it has been asked, can understand the mind of God, or who dare offer Him instruction? Well, at any rate, we share the standpoint of Christ.

III

Party Spirit

However, I could not speak to you, my brothers, as spiritually minded people, but only as earthbound, as mere babes in Christ. I fed you with milk, not with solid food; you were not capable of taking solids.

[3] And you are not yet capable; you are still worldly-minded. While there are jealousies and quarrels among you, are you not still worldly, and is not your behaviour just on the human level? When one says, 'I belong to Paul's party,' and another says, 'I follow Apollos,' are not you behaving like mere worldlings? After all, who is Paul, and who is Apollos? Just ministers by whose means you were brought to conversion. And whatever part each of us played was given him by the Lord. I planted, Apollos watered, but the growth came from God. Those who plant and water count for nothing in comparison with God, who alone can give capacity for growth. But the planter and the waterer have the same end in view, and each receives his reward in proportion to his toil, for you are God's garden and in it we work together with Him.

[10] To change the metaphor, I might say that you are God's house, which is now under construction. Like a wise architect, as God gave me grace, I laid a foundation. But somebody else builds on it. Well, let him be careful how he builds, for no one can lay any other foundation than the one that is already there, namely, Jesus Christ. And if anyone builds on that foundation a superstructure of any other material such as gold, silver, precious

stones, wood, hay, stubble, whatever it is will be made clear. The
Day of Judgment will show it up, when it is revealed by fire, and
the fire itself will assess the quality of each man's work. If anyone's superstructure survives he will be rewarded; if it is destroyed
he will be punished; and if he himself escapes, it will only be
through the flames of the burning building.

[16] Don't you realize that you are a temple of God, in which
the Spirit of God resides? If anyone destroys the temple of God,
God will destroy him. For the temple of God is holy, and that
means yourselves.

[18] Do not make any mistakes. If any one of you thinks he
knows a lot and is a man of the world, let him become a fool in
order to be truly wise. The wisdom of the world is folly in the
sight of God; as witness the two sentences from Scripture, 'He
outwits the clever in their cunning,' and 'The Lord knows the
arguments of the clever ones and how absurd they are.'

[21] So no mortal has any right to boast. You don't belong to
those leaders of whom you speak, but they belong to you. In
fact, everything belongs to you; Paul, Apollos, Cephas, the world
and life and death, and the present and the future—they are all
yours. And you belong to Christ as Christ belongs to God.

IV

As for us, you must look on us as servants of Christ and trustees
of God's revealed truth. The most necessary thing in a trustee is
that he should be trustworthy. As far as that is concerned, I don't
mind being examined by you or by any human court. I need not
even examine myself for I am not conscious of the least disloyalty.
But that does not altogether acquit me: I still await the Lord's
verdict.

[5] So do not pass any premature judgment, but wait until the
coming of the Lord. He will bring to light what is hidden in
darkness and will reveal even the intentions of the mind. Then
each man will receive his own appraisement from God.

[6]   All this, brothers, that I have said about Apollos and myself I will ask you to apply to your own case, so that you may learn the meaning of the instruction, 'Let no one exceed his commission.' Then you will not make ridiculous claims for one against another. Who has set you apart from anybody else? And what have you got that you did not receive from somebody? But if you received it, why should you boast as if you had made it yourself? You think you already have all you need, that you are already millionaires, that you are kings in your own right apart from us. Well, I wish you were in full possession of your kingdom, and then perhaps we could reign along with you. I think that God must have put us apostles last on the programme of the day's sport, like condemned criminals who are to meet their death in the arena. We have become a spectacle to the whole universe both of angels and of men. We are made to look fools for Christ's sake, while you are Christ's philosophers. We are weak, you are strong; you are looked up to, we are looked down upon. All this time we have been suffering hunger, thirst, lack of clothing, blows and utter destitution. We have to work hard, toiling with our own hands. Yet we return good words for evil; when we are persecuted we put up with it; we repay defamation with consolation. At this very moment we are like those poor wretches whom the authorities at Athens throw into the sea to represent the sins of the people—we are the world's cast-offs.

Forthcoming Visit

[14]   I am not writing this to put you in the wrong, but I am trying to advise you as if you were my own dear children. You may have thousands of teachers in Christ, but you haven't many fathers. It was I who was actually responsible for your birth in the gospel through Christ Jesus. Won't you then try to imitate me as children imitate their father? That is the reason why I have sent Timothy to you. He is my dear faithful son in the Lord and he will remind you of the way in which I tried to order my life after the pattern of Christ. That is the way I teach everywhere in every church.

[18]   Some people have been preening themselves, I hear, on the supposition that I shall not be visiting you in person. But I

shall come, and very soon, if God wills; and then I shall find out what these self-satisfied people are worth, not in verbosity, but in effectiveness. The Kingdom of God is not established by argument but by effective action. Which would you prefer, that I come to you with a big stick or in love and gentleness?

V

Church Discipline

There is a rumour that among you there has actually been committed incest, and such incest as is not practised even among the heathen—between a man and his step-mother. And you are still preening yourselves, instead of being full of grief until the man who has done such a thing has been driven out from among you. My own reaction is so strong that, although I am so far away, in imagination I am present with you and have passed sentence upon the man who perpetrated this crime—as if my spirit met with you in solemn assembly under the authority of our Lord Jesus Christ to deliver such a miscreant to Satan for the destruction of his body in order that at the Day of Judgment his soul may be saved. Your self-satisfaction is misplaced. Don't you know that a little yeast will permeate a whole baking of dough? Get rid of the old bad yeast, and make of yourselves new wholesome bread, we might almost say unleavened bread.

[7] The mention of unleavened bread reminds me of the Passover and of the Lamb. Christ is our Paschal Lamb, and He has already been offered for us. So then let us observe the feast in the customary way by not using the old yeast, the yeast of sin and wickedness, but by preparing the unleavened bread of sincerity and truth.

[9] I wrote to you in my last letter not to associate with immoral persons. I did not mean that you could avoid all contact with such people, or that you could never meet people who are lustful, rapacious or idolatrous. To do that you would have to leave the world altogether. But this letter is to bid you not to associate with any of our own brethren who has been convicted as immoral, lustful, idolatrous, abusive, drunken, or as a robber. You ought

never to sit at table with such people. It is no business of mine to pass judgment on non-Christians; but it is my business as well as yours to see that judgment is passed upon those who are within the Church. Those who are outside must be left to God's judgment. 'The evil person must be expelled from your company.'

VI

Litigation

When you have a case against another member of the Church, how dare you take it before a pagan court? Don't you realize that Christians will judge the whole world? If you are to judge the universe, are you incapable of judging the smallest matters? Don't you realize that we shall even judge the fallen angels? Much more then shall we judge human affairs. Well, when you have such affairs to adjudicate upon, do you set those who are of no account in the Church to act as arbitrators? I am saying this to arouse in you a sense of shame. Isn't there a single intelligent person among you who can act as arbitrator for the brotherhood? Has it come to this, that brother must drag brother into court and that before unbelievers? You have already lost your case by the very fact that you have lawsuits with one another. Why not rather suffer wrong? Why not rather let yourselves be robbed? You are actually the perpetrators of wrong and robbery, and that against the brethren. Don't you know that wrong-doers cannot inherit the Kingdom of God? Make no mistake about it. Immoral persons, idolators, adulterers, catamites, pederasts, thieves, avaricious people, drunkards, railers, robbers—none of these shall inherit the Kingdom of God. To their number you once belonged. But you were cleansed, acquitted, sanctified, in the name of our Lord Jesus Christ and in the Spirit of our God.

Licentiousness

[12] There are some who claim that as Christians they have a right to do anything. Perhaps, but not everything is fitting. 'To us,' they say, 'everything is lawful.' Perhaps, but as far as I am concerned, I will not let myself fall under the power of any bad

habit. 'Oh, well,' they retort, 'food is made for appetite and appetite for food.' Yes, but it is God who will one day destroy both. Surely the body is not made for immoral purposes but for the Lord, and the Lord rules over the body. God has raised the Lord's body and will raise us by the exercise of His power. Don't you know that your bodies are the limbs of Christ? Shall I then take the limbs of Christ and use them for a harlot? Perish the thought. Don't you know that he who has given himself to a prostitute has become one body with her? 'The two,' it says, 'shall become one flesh.' But he who gives himself to the Lord has become with Him one spirit. Avoid immorality. Sins are generally extraneous to the body, but the immoral person sins against his body. Don't you know that your body is the shrine of the Holy Spirit, who is in you and whom you receive from God? You do not belong to yourselves; you have been bought at a price. Then honour God in your body.

VII

Marriage and Celibacy

Now to touch on the points about which you specifically wrote to me. You ask whether celibacy is not the best condition of life. My answer is that in order to avoid immorality it is better for each man to have a wife of his own and for each woman to have a husband. The husband must fulfil his conjugal duty towards his wife and the wife must do the same for her husband. The wife's person is no longer her own, but her husband's, and the husband's no longer his own, but the wife's. Do not deprive one another of intercourse unless it is by agreement for a time in order to give greater attention to your prayers. And then come together again, or else Satan may tempt you through uncontrolled desire. But I say this by way of permission, not as a positive command. I wish everybody could be like myself, but all have their own gift from God, one for celibacy and another for marriage.

[8] To the unmarried and the widows I would say, 'It would be a good thing if, like me, you could stay as you are.' But if they are troubled by strong desire let them marry. Better to

marry than to feel oversexed. To the married I give a positive injunction (though it is not I that give it, but the Lord): The wife must not divorce her husband—if she does she must either remain unmarried or be reconciled to him. And the husband must not divorce his wife.

[12] To the rest I say (though there is no positive command of the Lord to this effect), if any of our brethren is married to a non-Christian and she is willing to continue living with him, he should not divorce her. Similarly, a woman married to a pagan should not divorce him if he is willing to remain with her. The unbelieving husband is sanctified by the believing wife and the unbelieving wife through her union with one of the brethren. Otherwise your children would be unsanctified, but actually they are baptized. But if the Pagan partner prefers to separate, don't forbid it. The Christian brother or sister is not bound by the marriage bond in such cases. You were living at peace when God called you, and how can you tell, dear sister, whether you will not save your husband, or you, dear brother, whether you will not save your wife?

[17] Apart from that, it is a good general rule that each should continue to live in the condition in which God apportioned him his lot or his calling. That is the principle I lay down in all the churches. So, for instance, those who belonged to the ranks of the circumcised when they received their call should not try to disguise the fact. Similarly, those who were not circumcised have no need to be so. Circumcision and uncircumcision have no importance whatever: the important thing is to keep God's commandments. So let each remain in the condition in which he was when he was called.

[21] Similarly again, if you were a slave when you were called, don't worry about it. Even if you find it possible to become free, be easy about it. He who is called as a slave to serve the Lord is the Lord's freedman, and the man who is called in freedom is Christ's slave. You have been purchased at a price: don't become any man's slave. Brothers, each of you, now that you serve God, must remain in the condition in which you were called.

[25]   On the subject of Virgins I have no instructions from the
Lord, but I give you my own opinion as that of one whom by the
mercy of God you can trust. I reckon then that in view of the
impending Judgment it is good for a man to remain as he is.
Are you bound by the bonds of matrimony? Don't try to loose
them. Are you single? Don't try to marry. But if you marry, you
have committed no sin. Similarly, if the Virgin in your household
marry, she commits no sin. But such will have harassing cares
and I would spare you those. I assure you, brothers, that time is
short. It follows that those who have wives should live as though
they had none, those in mourning as though they had no time
for tears, those in jubilation as though they had no time to cele-
brate, buyers as though they had purchased nothing, and society
people as though they never went out. For this world and all its
concerns are merely transitory.

[32]   I should like to keep you free from care. The single man
gives himself to the Lord's business, anxious only to please Him.
The married man has to attend to mundane affairs and is
anxious to please his wife: his is a divided allegiance. Similarly
girls and unmarried women give themselves to the Lord's business and are anxious to maintain their purity both of body and
spirit, but the married woman has to attend to household affairs
and is anxious to please her husband. I am saying all this for
your good, not just in order to restrict your freedom, but to
secure for you an opportunity to live a life of complete purity
and devotion to the Lord.

[36]   At the same time, if anyone has a Virgin in his house and
thinks he is not treating her properly, and if his desire is strong
and things are otherwise fitting, let him do as he pleases, he
commits no sin if they marry. But he who remains firm and
steadfast in his original intention, suffering under no necessity of
passion, and decides that as far as the decision lies with him he
will keep his Virgin in strict continency, does well. He who
decides to marry his Virgin does well too, but he who decides
not to marry will do better.

[39]   A wife is bound in wedlock for so long a time as her husband
is alive, but if he dies she is free to marry whom she will, so long

as he is a Christian.   But in my opinion she is happier if she
remain as she is.   And that, I believe, is a view prompted by the
Spirit of God.

VIII

Meat offered to Idols

Regarding now the question of eating food which has been
sacrificed to idols : we know, as you said, that we are all in a
position to express our views on that matter.   But that kind of
knowledge is likely to make us conceited, whereas mutual love
will improve our character.   If a man really possesses knowledge,
he ought to recognize that he still does not know anything sufficiently well.   But if a man loves God, he has at least been himself
an object of knowledge to God (and that is better than having
any knowledge of our own).

[4]   Well then, on this question of eating meat which has been
used in Pagan sacrifices, we know that an idol is really nothing
at all, and that actually there is only one God.   Although there
are things that are called gods both in the sky and on the earth—
although there are in fact many so-called gods and lords—yet
they are nothing to us who acknowledge only one God the Father,
from whom all things proceed and for whom we exist, and one
Lord Jesus Christ by whose agency everything came into being
including ourselves.

[7]   However, not everyone possesses this knowledge.   Consequently some who have had previous acquaintance with idol-
worship and still eat food that has formed part in it, put a burden
of scruple on their conscience.   But food will not commend us to
God.   As far as He is concerned, we are none the better if we eat
and none the worse if we refrain from eating.   But take care that
your authority in this respect does not become a stumbling-block
to the scrupulous.   If anyone sees you who are reputed to be
'wise' sitting at table in an idol-house, he is likely to be encouraged himself to eat food that has been offered to idols.   And is
that really calculated to 'strengthen his weak conscience'?   It
would be terrible for your knowledge to destroy the weak,

especially when you remember that he is a brother for whom
Christ died. By thus sinning against the brethren and wounding
their scrupulous conscience you sin against Christ. So if the eating
of such meat is a source of offence to my brother, rather than
offend him I will become a downright vegetarian for as long as
I live.

IX

The Rights of an Apostle

It is true that I personally am free to do as I like, that I am an
Apostle, and that I have seen Jesus our Lord. Are not you yourselves evidence of my work for the Lord? If I am not an apostle
to anyone else, I certainly am to you. You are the very confirmation of my apostleship in the Lord. My defence to those who
criticise me is as follows:

[4] Have I no right to do as I like in the matter of eating and
drinking? Have I no right to take to myself a wife from among
our sisters like the other apostles and the Lord's brothers and
Peter? Are Barnabas and I the only ones who have no right to
give up our trade and be kept by the Church?

[7] What soldier on campaign ever supplied his own rations?
Who ever planted a vineyard without expecting to enjoy the
grapes? What shepherd minds a flock and does not refresh himself from its milk? But I need not draw out these human
analogies; does not the Divine law say the same? In the Mosaic
law it is written: 'Thou shalt not muzzle the ox that thresheth
the grain.' Is it of the oxen that God is thinking, or isn't it true
that the major reference is to us? It is for us that the command
was written, because the ploughman needs to plough in hope and
the thresher should expect to share the grain.

[11] If we have sown spiritual seed for you, is it a great thing
that we should harvest some of your material goods? If others
share this right over you, surely we possess it to a greater extent.
You say we did not seize our opportunity. No, because we do
not mind what we suffer so long as we put no obstacle in the way

of the gospel of Christ. Need I remind you that even the Temple ministers get their living out of the Temple and that attendants at the altar get a share of the sacrifices? Even so has the Lord ordered that they who minister the Gospel shall live by the Gospel.

[15] But I have used none of those opportunities, and I am not writing now in order to avail myself of them. I would rather die than—well, at any rate, no one shall rob me of my proudest boast. What I am really proud about is not just the preaching of the Gospel; I am absolutely obliged to do that, I couldn't live without doing it. If I do it willingly, I have my reward; even if I do it unwillingly I am still discharging my trust. What then is my reward? Just this. That I may do my preaching without cost to anyone. By that means I refrain from exercising the right I enjoy in the Gospel.

[19] Though I am a free agent and not bound to anyone, I make myself everybody's slave in order that I may win the more. To the Jews I become a Jew that I may win the Jews. To those who observe the Mosaic Law I become subject to the Law (although I am not actually bound by it) in order that I may win the law-keepers. To those who are outside the Law I become a law-breaker (although I am not really a breaker of the Divine Law, but an observer of the Christian Law) in order that I may win those who are outside the Law. To those worried by many scruples I become scrupulous in order that I may win the scrupulous. I am all things to all men in order that by all means I may save some.

[23] Everything I do is for the Gospel's sake that I may make sure of my own share in it. You know how in a race all the competitors run, but only one wins the prize. You should run in such a way as to make sure of being prize-winners. Everyone who enters for an athletic contest goes into training and exercises self-discipline in everything. They do it to obtain a perishable trophy, we do it to obtain an everlasting crown. So I run with a goal clear before me; I fight not like a man who is shadow-boxing, but against an opponent whom I actually hit and bruise, namely, my own body, which I reduce to complete subjection. After all

4

my preaching to others I must leave no possibility of being
rejected myself.

X

Sacraments, Jewish, Christian and Pagan

I should like you to realize, brothers, that when our ancestors
journeyed under the cloud and all passed through the sea, they
were all in a sense baptized in the water of the cloud and of the
sea. Similarly they all ate one supernatural food and drank one
supernatural drink. For they drank from a supernatural rock
that followed them and that Rock was Christ. But with the
majority of them God was displeased and they perished in the
desert.

[6] These things happened as warnings to us that we should not
give way to evil passions as they did. Nor must you become idol-
worshippers, as were some of them. You remember the line,
'The people sat down to eat and drink, and rose to mischief.'
Nor must we give way to immorality as did some of them, with
the result that as many as 23,000 perished in one day. Nor must
we try the patience of God as some of them did and were killed
by snakes. And do not grumble as did some of them, only to
perish at the hands of the Destroying Angel.

[11] These things happened to them by way of warning to
others, and they have been recorded for our instruction who are
living near the end of the world. Let anyone who imagines he
is safe take care that he is not tripped up. You have not so far
been waylaid by any temptation that is not common to all
humanity. God is to be relied upon: He will not let you be
tempted above your capacity to resist. When He allows you to
be tempted He will always provide some way out of it, so that
you need not be overcome.

[14] So, my dear people, avoid all worship connected with idols.
I am talking to wise men; see if I am not right. We have our own
sacred meal. In it is the cup over which a blessing is pronounced:
is not that our way of sharing in the Blood of Christ? The bread

that we break, is not that a sharing in the Body of Christ? Although we are many we thus become one loaf, one body, because we all share in the one loaf.

[18] Compare the case of the Jewish people. Are not they who eat the meat offered in their sacrifices sharers in the same altar? Well, you may ask, what does that imply? That it is of any importance that certain meat has been offered to an idol? Or that an idol itself is anything at all? No, simply that when Pagans offer sacrifice, they do it not to God, but to demons. I don't want you to share in the character of demons. You can't at the same time drink the chalice of the Lord and that of demons; you can't participate in the table of the Lord and that of demons. Do we want to make the Lord jealous? Are we stronger than He? No doubt everything is allowable for Christians: yes, but not everything is expedient. Everything is allowable; but everything does not promote edification. We must not pursue our own advantage but that of the other fellow.

[25] Whatever you buy in the market, eat it, and don't ask any questions about its origin or the use it has already served, and then your conscience will not be hurt. 'The earth is the Lord's and all that is in it.' Similarly, if you are invited out by an unbeliever and wish to go, eat whatever is put before you, asking no questions, and so maintain a quiet conscience. But if anyone says to you, 'This food has been used in idol worship,' then don't eat it, both for the sake of him who drew your attention to it and also for conscience sake—not your conscience, of course, but that of the other fellow.

[29] 'But,' you say, 'why should my freedom be at the beck and call of somebody else's conscience? If I say grace first, why should I be charged in respect of something over which a blessing has been asked?' Well, the answer is, whatever you do, eating or drinking or anything else, do it all for the glory of God. Don't put a stumbling-block in anyone's way whether Jew or Greek or Christian. Personally, I try to satisfy everybody on every point. I don't pursue my own advantage, but that of the public, with a view to their salvation. In this respect you had better imitate me as I imitate Christ.

XI

Public Worship

I congratulate you on the way you have kept my advice in mind and held fast the traditions as I handed them on to you. I should now like you to bear in mind that while Christ is the head of every man, the head of every woman is her husband, just as the head of Christ is God. It follows that if a man prays or prophesies with his hat on his head he shows a lack of respect to that Head which is Christ. Conversely, every woman who prays or prophesies with head uncovered dishonours her head: she might just as well have her head shaved. If a woman won't wear her veil in church, she should cut off her hair; but if it is a disgrace to a woman to be shorn or shaven, then let her be veiled. A man ought not to cover his head, for he is the image and glory of God, but woman is man's glory. Man was not derived from woman, but woman from man, and man was not originally created by means of woman, but woman by means of man. So woman ought to bear some sign of submission to authority on her head, or else what will the angels think? This does not mean that there is any conflict between man and woman. They are complementary in the Christian life: neither is anything without the other. As woman originally proceeded from man, so does man now come into existence by means of woman; but both alike come from God.

[13] Use your common sense. Is it fitting that a woman should say her prayers with her head uncovered? Doesn't nature herself teach that long hair is a disgrace to a man, but a glory to a woman. Obviously her hair is given her for a covering. However, if anyone disagrees, all I can say to him is that we have no such custom, nor has any of the churches of God.

[17] In giving advice on this matter, I have a more definite cause of complaint. You are diverting your assemblies from their true purpose. In the first place, I hear that when you come together as a congregation, there are disagreements among you,

and I am half-inclined to believe it. I suppose there must be some divisions of opinion among you in order that the true and tried among you may be made obvious to all.

[20] That explains why, when you gather together, it is not really to partake of the Lord's Supper. At your meal each one brings his own supper, with the result that while one goes hungry another drinks too much. Haven't you got homes of your own in which to eat and drink? Or do you wish to show contempt for the church of God and put the poor to shame? What am I to say? Find you a few words of congratulation? I certainly shall not congratulate you on that score. The traditional manner of conducting this service, which I handed on to you, I actually had on the Lord's own authority. I was taught how the Lord Jesus on the night when He was betrayed took bread and gave thanks and brake it and said, 'This is my Body which is given for you: do this as a memorial of me.' Similarly, after supper He took the cup and said, 'This cup is the new agreement signed in my blood: offer this as often as you drink it for a memorial of me.' Whenever then you eat this Loaf and drink this Cup you proclaim the Lord's death until He comes.

[27]   It follows that if anyone eats the Bread or drinks the Cup in an irreverent manner he will be guilty in respect of the Body and Blood of the Lord. Let a man make up his mind and then let him eat of the Loaf and drink of the Cup. He who partakes of this food without recognizing it as the Body eats and drinks to his own condemnation. For this reason many among you are weak and sickly and some are just spiritual corpses. But if we judge ourselves we shall not be judged. Even as it is, when we are judged by the Lord we are corrected in order that we may not be condemned with the world. So then, my brothers, when you come together to eat, wait for one another: if anyone is hungry let him eat at home, in order that when you meet together it may not involve your condemnation. The rest I will arrange when I come.

XII

Spiritual Gifts

I do not want you to go ignorant of the true nature of spiritual gifts. You know how, when you were Pagans, you were subject to the influence of dumb idols. So now a man's utterances will reflect the influence of the spirit that moves him. If he says, 'Cursed be Jesus,' he cannot be speaking under the impulse of the Spirit of God, and conversely it is only under the influence of the Holy Spirit that one can really say, 'Jesus is Lord.' Of course there is a variety of gifts, but only one Spirit; and there is a variety of opportunities for service, but only one Lord, and there is a variety of manifestations of spiritual power, but it is the same God who manifests His power in each and all.

[7] But the Spirit is manifested in each one individually for some specific purpose. To one through the Spirit is revealed a store of practical wisdom, to another by the same Spirit is granted intellectual understanding, to another faith by the same Spirit, to another gifts of healing by the same Spirit, to another psychological powers, to another prophecy, to another capacity to distinguish between good and bad spirits, to another various kinds of ecstatic utterance, to another the power to interpret such utterances. But all these gifts are derived from the impulses of the same identical Spirit, who distributes to each recipient just as He wishes.

[12] As our body is one entity and yet is made up of a number of limbs, and all the limbs join together to make up only one body, so it is with Christ. We were all baptized in one Spirit into one Body, whether Jews or Greeks, whether slaves or free men, and we have all imbibed one Spirit. The body is not one limb but many. If the foot were to say, 'I am not a hand and therefore I do not belong to the body,' it would still be part of the body. And if the ear were to say, 'I am not an eye and therefore I do not belong to the body,' it would still be part of the body. If the whole body were an eye, how could you hear? And if the whole were an ear, how could we smell? But as things are, God has appointed limbs for the body, each of them performing the

functions He has assigned. If the whole were just one limb, what would the body be? Actually there are many limbs and only one body. The eye cannot say to the hand, 'I have no need of you'; nor can the head say to the feet, 'I have no need of you.' On the contrary, those members of the body that seem especially frail are the most necessary. The less noble parts, too, are compensated by being covered with clothes which adorn even while they conceal, and our very modesty gives to the less seemly parts a decorousness of which the more seemly parts have no lack. God has so constructed the body, giving dignity to those parts that lacked it, in order that there should be no schism in the body, but that the limbs should have the more care for each other. If one limb aches, all the others ache in sympathy, and if one limb is specially honoured, all the others share the honour.

[27] You are the body of Christ and its individual limbs. God has given each his own place in the Church, first apostles, second prophets, third teachers, then miracle-workers, then those who have gifts of healing, of general helpfulness, of administration, of speaking in a variety of ecstatic utterances. Is everyone an apostle? Is everyone a prophet? Is everyone a teacher? Is everyone a worker of miracles? Has everyone the gift of healing? Can everyone speak in ecstasy? Can everyone interpret? You should try to cultivate the more useful gifts. But I can show you an even better way than that, the way of love.

XIII

The Best Gift

Supposing I could speak in ecstasy with the languages of all the different races of men and even with those of the different orders of angels, all my words would be as empty of meaning as beaten brass or clanging cymbals, if I did not possess the gift of love. Even though I were a prophet and could penetrate every mystery and was versed in every sphere of knowledge, and though I had all faith so that I could remove mountains, and had not love, I should be nothing. And even if I doled out all my possessions in gifts of food, or flung myself on a fire in self-immolation, and had not love, I should be in no way benefited.

[4]   Love is patient; love is kind; love makes no parade, refrains
from boasting, never lacks courtesy, never pursues its own selfish
interest, never shows bitterness or resentment, never takes
pleasure in wickedness but only in the truth. Love keeps its own
counsel, shows a ready trust, is full of hope and sturdy perseverance. Love never falls down on its task. Prophecies sometimes
prove false; ecstatic utterances sometimes lack sense; knowledge
sometimes makes mistakes. After all, our knowledge is only
partial and our prophecies but half-truths. But when perfection
comes all that is incomplete is superseded. When I was a child
I used to talk like a child, think like a child, argue like a child.
But when I grew up to man's estate I dropped my childish ways.
In our present condition it is as though we were peering into a
defective mirror and seeing everything distorted, but then we
shall look straight at reality. Now my knowledge is but partial,
but then I shall know as I myself am known. So then there
remain these three gifts, faith, hope and love, and the best of all
is love.

XIV

Superiority of Prophecy over 'Tongues'

First make sure of love and then try for spiritual gifts and
especially that of prophecy. He who speaks in ecstasy speaks not
to men but to God. No one listens to him, although in his own
spirit he may be giving utterance to revealed truths. On the
other hand, he who prophesies speaks words that bring to others
edification, courage and comfort. He who speaks in a 'tongue'
edifies himself, but he who prophesies edifies the Church. I
should be glad if you all spoke with tongues, but I would rather
you prophesied. The prophet is more useful than the ecstatic—
unless, of course, the latter is capable of interpreting his own
utterances in such a way as to instruct the Church. So now,
brothers, if I come to you giving frequent utterance to ecstatic
tongues, what good shall I do you, unless I speak to you by way
of revelation, or instruction, or prophecy or teaching?

[7]   Take the case of such inanimate things as produce sounds,
like a flute or a harp, if it makes no difference between its various

sounds how can the flautist or harpist make his tune understood? If when a trumpet is blown no one can recognize the call, who will ever leap to arms? So with yourselves, if you speak indistinctly, how can what you say be understood? You will be speaking to the air. It so happens that there are in existence many different kinds of language, and everything has its own characteristic mode of expression. But if I don't understand the significance of the sound made, I shall be a barbarian to the speaker and the speaker a barbarian to me.

[12] So don't make that mistake, but as you are anxious for spiritual gifts cultivate those especially that tend to the edification of the Church. If anyone has a gift for ecstatic utterance, let him pray for the gift of interpretation. If I pray in ecstasy my spirit prays but my understanding derives no benefit. Well, then, I should like to pray not only with the spirit, but also with the understanding. Even if I sing in the spirit, I should like to sing with the mind as well.

[16] The reason for all this is obvious. If it is in the spirit that you deliver a blessing over the Eucharist, how will anyone who is a member of the congregation say the Amen at the end of your thanksgiving? He won't be able to understand what you say. You may render the thanksgiving beautifully, but the other won't be helped by it. Thank God, I do more speaking in ecstasy than any of you, but in church I would rather speak five words with my understanding than thousands in ecstasy.

[20] Brothers, don't be childish—except where evil is concerned, but in intelligence try to be your age. In the Law it is written. Thus saith the Lord, 'In foreign tongues and with the lips of foreigners will I speak to my People, and even so they will not listen to me.' So you see these strange utterances are not meant as a sign for believers, but for unbelievers. Prophecy on the other hand is not for unbelievers but for the faithful. If, however, the whole church is assembled for worship and everyone is speaking in ecstasy and ignorant or hostile people come in, won't they say that you are just mad? But if everyone is prophesying and an unbelieving or ignorant person comes in, he will be convinced and answered by all; his most secret thoughts and emotions will

be made clear, and he will fall down on his knees and do obeisance to God, crying out, 'Truly God is with you.'

[26] Well then, brothers, when you come to meeting, each one of you has something to contribute, a hymn or a piece of instruction, or a revelation, or an ecstatic utterance, or an interpretation. Let everything be done with a view to edification. If you speak in ecstasy, let only two or at the most three do it, and that in turns, and let one explain the meaning of what they say. But if there is no one present capable of giving an explanation, let the ecstatics keep silence and speak only to themselves and God. Let the prophets speak two or three at a meeting, and let the rest exercise their power of discrimination between them. If while one is speaking something is suddenly revealed to another who is sitting down, let the first be silent. You can all prophesy one at a time, and then everyone will have a chance of learning something and being helped. The prophetic spirit is surely under the control of the prophets. God does not create confusion, but ordered peace.

[34] There is in this connection another custom which is universal in the Christian Church. It is that women should observe silence in the congregation. Women are not allowed to speak in public worship. As the Law expressly states, they should refrain from pushing themselves forward. If they wish to be enlightened on any topic, they should consult their husbands at home. It is not seemly for a woman to speak in church. If you don't like this ruling, I must remind you that the word of God did not originate with you, nor are you the only ones who have received it.

[37] If anyone thinks he is a prophet or endowed with spiritual gifts, let him recognize that what I have written to you comes as a commandment of the Lord. If he won't recognize it, give him no recognition himself. To sum it all up, my brothers, cultivate earnestly the gift of prophecy, while not forbidding ecstatic utterance. But let everything be done in a seemly and orderly fashion.

XV

The Resurrection

May I remind you, brothers, of the precise nature of the 'good news' I proclaimed to you. You accepted that gospel of mine; on it you took your stand; and by it you are even now being saved—if you stick to my version of it—unless your belief was merely idle. Well then, I delivered to you what I myself had received at first hand, that Christ in fulfilment of the Scriptures died for our sins, that He was buried, that three days afterwards as the Scriptures had foretold He was raised again, and that He was seen first by Cephas, then by the Twelve, after that by more than five hundred of the brethren all at the same time (most of them are still alive, but some of them are dead); after that again He was seen by James and by the whole body of the Apostles. Last of all He was seen by me—your poor little runt of an apostle. I am indeed the least of the Apostles, and hardly deserve the name of Apostle, because I once persecuted the Church of God. But I owe it to the grace of God that I am what I am, and the favour that He showed me was not wasted, but my toil has produced even greater results than that of all the others. Yet it was not I that did it, but the grace of God that was with me. Anyhow, whether it was I or they, the above are the terms in which we preached and those are the terms in which you believed.

[12] But if Christ is preached as having been raised from the dead, how comes it that some of you say there is no such thing as a resurrection of the dead? If there is no resurrection of the dead, then Christ was not raised. But if Christ was not raised then there is nothing real in our preaching or in your faith. And we are exposed as perjured witnesses of God, because we gave you our testimony with regard to Him that He raised up Christ—and He certainly did not raise Him if the dead do not rise. If the dead do not rise, then Christ was not raised; but if Christ was not raised, your faith has effected nothing: you are still in your sins, and the faithful who have already departed this life have passed clean out of existence. But if our hopes in Christ are limited to this life we are the most miserable of all men.

[20] However, we know that Christ has been raised from the dead and has become as it were the first sheaf of the whole harvest of the gathered dead. Just as it was through a man that death came into the world, so through a man has come the resurrection of the dead. As in Adam everyone is doomed to die, so in Christ shall all be made alive. But each in his proper order; Christ is the first fruits, and when He appears the Christian dead will be raised. Then will come the end of the world, when He will hand over the Kingdom to God, even the Father, and annihilate every demonic Rule, Authority and Power. He will have to maintain the rule Himself until He has brought all His foes into subjection. The last enemy to be destroyed will be death. 'God,' we are told, 'made the whole universe subject to Him.' (When it says 'the whole universe', it is obvious that it does not include God Himself, who was responsible for bringing about this subjection of the whole universe to Him.) After the subjection of the universe has been finally completed, then the Son will place Himself last of all under God through whom He has attained His own supremacy. Thus God will be all in all.

[29] Otherwise what would happen in the case of people baptized as proxies on behalf of those candidates for baptism who have died before they could receive the sacrament? If the departed are not raised, what is the good of being baptized for them? And for the matter of that, why do I put myself in jeopardy every hour? I swear by your pride in me, which I cherish so much in Christ Jesus our Lord, I do die every day in voluntary suffering and self-denial. What advantage would it be to me that I have fought at Ephesus with men who are little better than wild beasts? If the dead are not raised, why not follow the old Epicurean maxim, 'Let us eat and drink, for to-morrow we die.' Don't make that mistake, for the best of dispositions can be spoilt by evil suggestions. Be sensitive to goodness and don't fall into sin. Some of you unfortunately have no awareness of God. I remind you of the fact to move you to shame.

[35] But someone will say, 'How are the dead raised up and with what kind of body will they appear?' Stupid. The ordinary seed you sow does not germinate unless it first dies. And when you sow seed, you do not actually sow the future body, but just

simple grain, either wheat or some other kind. God gives it the body He has designed for it, and to each seed a characteristic body of its own. Similarly with animal bodies, their flesh is not all the same, but there is one kind that is characteristic of human beings, another of animals, another of birds and another of fishes. So also heavenly bodies are distinguished from earthly: either type has a splendour of its own. And further, the heavenly bodies differ among themselves. The splendour of the sun is different from that of the moon, and both from that of the stars. And even each star has a splendour different from that of its fellows.

[42] The resurrection of the dead is just like that. What is sown is perishable; what is raised is imperishable. What is sown is second-rate; what is raised is glorious. What is sown is weak; what is raised is strong. What is sown is a physical body; what is raised is a spiritual body. Just as there is a physical body, so there is a spiritual body. That is the meaning of the passage, 'The first man, Adam, received the gift of physical life; the Second Adam was Himself a life-giving spirit.'

[45] The spiritual does not come first but the physical, and then the spiritual. The First Man belongs to the earth and is a material being; the Second Man is from heaven. To the pattern of the material man belong all material men, and to the pattern of the Heavenly Man belong all who are of Heaven. As we were made like the material man, so shall we become like the Heavenly Man. But this I affirm, brethren, that flesh and blood cannot inherit the Kingdom of God, neither can what is mortal inherit immortality. I will explain the mystery: we shall not all die, but we shall be changed, in a moment, in the twinkling of an eye, at the last trumpet call. For the trumpet will sound, and the dead will be raised immortal, while we who are still alive will be transformed.

[54] When this mortality has thus clothed itself with immortality and this perishable nature of ours with imperishability, then the passage will be fulfilled where it is written, 'Death is swallowed up in victory'. O death, where is now your victory, and where, O death, your sting? The sting of death lies in our sin, and our sin receives its poignancy from the Law. But thanks be to God,

who through our Lord Jesus Christ, has bestowed on us the victory over both.

[58] So then, my beloved brothers, be steadfast, unfaltering; multiply your efforts on the Lord's behalf, for now you see that your labour cannot fail when it is linked with that of Christ.

XVI

Personal

With regard to the collection of alms for our fellow-Christians: you will please follow the same procedure that I laid down for the churches of Galatia. Each first day of the week let everyone set aside something from his earnings and save it up so that we may not have to make any special appeals when I come. And then when I arrive, whomsoever you appoint I will send with letters to take your gift to Jerusalem. If the sum is sufficiently important to warrant me going myself, they shall go with me.

[5] I will come to you when I have completed my tour through Macedonia. I must put in an appearance there, and then perhaps I shall stay with you and even pass the winter with you. Afterwards you can set me on my way wherever I go. I don't want to call in on you now, for I should like to spend some time with you, if it be God's will. In any case, I am staying at Ephesus till Pentecost, for the door of opportunity is wide open for me here with a good chance of effective work in spite of much opposition.

[10] If Timothy comes, see that he suffers no embarrassment, for he is on the Lord's duty, as I am, and is not to be looked down upon. Set him on his way peaceably so that he may come on to me, for I am expecting him to come with the other brothers.

[12] As for brother Apollos, I have strongly urged him to come to you with the others. Only he does not want to come just now, but he will come at a more suitable time.

[13] Keep on the alert; stand fast in the faith; show a manly courage; be strong. Let everything you do be steeped in love. One special request, brothers: you know the household of Stephanas, how it was the first in Achaia to be converted and

how its members have spent themselves in ministering to the faithful. Well, give all the help you can to such friends and to everyone who works and toils at our common task.

[17] I rejoice in the arrival of Stephanas, Fortunatus and Achaicus, for they compensate for my loss of your company. They have relieved my mind and yours: such should receive proper recognition.

[19] The churches of Asia send you greetings; Aquila and Priscilla send specially warm greetings together with the congregation that meets in their house. All the brethren greet you; salute one another with the kiss of peace. I send you my own greetings in my own handwriting and sign them

Paul.

Postscript

[22] Avoid those who have no love for the Lord. 'Come, Lord, come.' The grace of the Lord Jesus be with you. My love to you all in Christ Jesus.

S. Paul's Second Letter
To The Corinthians

From Paul, appointed Apostle by the will of God, and from Timothy, his brother in the faith, to the Church of God in Corinth and to all Christian people throughout Achaia: grace to you and peace from God our Father and our Lord Jesus Christ.

Introduction

[3] Blessed be the God and Father of our Lord Jesus Christ, the Father of compassion and the God of all comfort. He comforts us in all our afflictions, and so enables us to comfort others who are in any trouble with the same comfort that we ourselves have received from Him. As I have shared liberally in Christ's sufferings, so I share liberally in His comfort. Therefore if I am afflicted, it is for your comfort and salvation; if I am comforted, it is in order that I may hand on to you such comfort as will enable you to endure the same sufferings that I suffer. So my hope for you is well-founded, for I know that as you share my sufferings, so you share also my comfort.

[8] I don't wish to disguise from you, brothers, the fact that when the trouble happened to me in Asia I was so utterly crushed as to despair even of life. However, I was allowed to believe that I was under sentence of death only in order that I should learn not to trust in myself but in God who raises the dead. On that occasion He rescued me from death, and He will continue to rescue me. Yes, and I hope He will be my rescuer while you combine your common efforts in prayer on my behalf. Thus as a result of many people's co-operation a great body of thanksgiving will be offered to Him on my behalf for the boon He has conferred upon me.

Vindication of Recent Actions

[12] It is my proud boast (and my conscience is in full agreement with it), that I have behaved myself in society generally and especially in your regard with holiness and godly sincerity, not showing much knowledge of the world but plenty of the grace of God. I am writing to you without ambiguity and without suggesting anything more than my words actually convey or than you already know and will, I trust, continue to realize right to the end. You already have some knowledge of me and I hope you will approve of me as I shall of you in the Day of our Lord Jesus Christ.

[15] Confident as I was about all this, I should have liked to visit you twice before and to have given you the pleasure of my company. The first time would have been when you might have set me on my way to Macedonia, the second when I returned from Macedonia and you might have set me on my way to Judea. Do you think I made those plans light-heartedly, or that when I make plans for the conduct of business I leave myself free to change them at will? As God Himself is trustworthy, I swear to you that my promise was definite and firm. Christ Jesus, whom we, that is Silvanus, Timotheus and myself, proclaimed to you as Son of God, is not changeable, and the decision rests with Him. He actually confirms all the promises of God. That is why, when we are at worship, we add an Amen in His name to the glory of God. It is God who has anointed both us and you and confirmed us in our relation to Christ, and He has also set His seal upon us and given us the token of His Spirit in our hearts.

The Change of Plan

[23] But I swear to you as God is my witness that the reason why I abandoned my visit to Corinth was simply that I wished to spare you embarrassment. You see I don't domineer over you in matters of faith, but I co-operate with you to ensure your happiness. In matters of faith you are able to stand on your own feet.

II

I decided that I would avoid coming to you a second time in painful circumstances. For if I were to cause you pain, where should I look for joy except among those whom I had thus made sad? That is why I wrote in that fashion, so that when I do come I shall not be pained by those from whom I hope to receive nothing but joy. For I know you well enough to be sure that you all take pleasure in giving pleasure to me.

The Point of the last Letter

[4] It was in great distress and heartfelt sorrow that I wrote to you, and with many tears, not in order to give you pain but to let you know the overwhelming love I bear you. The man who has caused such grief has done it not to me only but in a measure (I don't want to exaggerate) to all of you. Enough for him is the judgment passed upon him by the majority. Now you can relent and forgive him and comfort him. You don't want him to be overwhelmed by excessive remorse. So I beg you to exercise some kindness towards him.

[9] That is why I wrote, to test you and to see whether you are thoroughly obedient. If you register an act of pardon, I endorse it. Whatever pardon I myself have granted, I did it for your sakes and as representative of Christ, and also to prevent Satan taking advantage of your difficult position, for I know something about his devices.

How he has fared elsewhere

[12] When I came to Troas to preach the gospel of Christ, the Lord opened wide a door of opportunity for me, but I was very disturbed at not finding brother Titus; so I left them and went on to Macedonia. But thank God, my journey turned out to be a triumphal procession everywhere. (God made it so through Christ.) Not even the processional incense was wanting, for through me He diffused the fragrance of His knowledge in every place. Indeed we ourselves are the divine fragrance of Christ

both for those who are being saved and for those who are perishing. For the latter we are a noxious odour that hastens their death, but for the former a refreshing perfume that renews their life.

[17] How can anyone be big enough for such a task? At any rate I am not like those, the majority I am afraid, who are mere peddlers of the word of God. I am at least sincere, and I speak in Christ as one divinely inspired before the very presence of God.

III

Digression on the Ministry

But I must not start trying to justify myself again. Surely I don't need, like the rest, letters of commendation either to you or from you. You are my letter, written on my heart, open for anyone to read, clearly a letter of Christ's written by me at His dictation, not in ink but in the Spirit of the Living God, not on tablets of stone but on the living tablets of the heart.

[4] You see what confidence Christ gives me in my relation to God. Not that I am able to reckon anything to my own credit, but my credit comes from God, who has credited me with the ministry of the New Agreement. And that agreement is based not on written law but on the Spirit. The difference is that the Law punishes with death, but the Spirit brings to life. But even that ministry of death, engraved in writing on stone, was brought into existence with a great blaze of glory, and transient as it was, Moses was so radiant from his contact with it, that the Israelites could not bear to let their eyes rest upon his face. If that was the case then, will not the ministry of the Spirit reflect an infinitely greater Glory? For if it is a glorious thing to administer penalties, a ministry of acquittal must be much more glorious. The splendour of the former was only partial in comparison with the splendour of the latter which superseded it. And if the transient had its element of splendour, then the permanent must be much more splendid.

The Candour of the Gospel

[12] Inspired with such confidence I am quite open with you, and have no need, as Moses had, to hide his face with a veil and so disguise from the Israelites the impermanence of his radiance. In any case they were too set in their prejudices, so that even to-day the same veil hangs over their understanding of the Old Agreement. It has not been removed, although as a matter of fact Christ has made it useless. But down to the present moment whenever the books of Moses are read a veil lies over their minds. The moment they turn to the Lord that veil will be taken away. The Lord is the Spirit, and where the Lord's Spirit is there is freedom. As for us who gaze with unveiled face on the glory of the Lord, we shall all be changed from one glory to another under the influence of the Lord the Spirit until we are transformed into His likeness.

IV

The Light of the Gospel

And so, as I have been given a ministry in this new order, in accordance with the mercy shown me I refuse to despair. I will have nothing to do with secret and shameful practices; I exercise no duplicity; I do not falsify the gospel teaching; but by simply stating the truth I commend myself to the judgment of every man's conscience in the sight of God.

[3] If my gospel is 'veiled', it is veiled only to those who are on the road to destruction. The god of this world has blinded the eyes of unbelievers so that they shall not see the light of the glorious gospel of Christ, who is the likeness of God. I do not preach about myself, but about Christ as Lord, and about myself as your servant on account of Him. The God who said, 'Let there be light,' has Himself shined in my heart to reveal the knowledge of His own glory in the face of Christ.

[7] But the casket in which I carry my treasure is no 'strong box'. And that at least makes it obvious that the transcendent power is not mine but God's. I suffer every kind of affliction, but

I am not overwhelmed; I am often at a loss, but never in despair; I am persecuted, but not deserted; beaten to my knees, but not finished off; always carrying about in my own body the death of Jesus in order that the life also of Jesus may be displayed in my person. It is always happening that we who are truly alive are delivered up to death for Jesus' sake in order that the life of Jesus may be made visible in our mortal flesh.

[12] So death is active in me but life in you. However, we have the same spirit of faith. And you know how it is written, 'I believed and therefore I had to speak'; so I believe and am under the same constraint to speak. I know that He who raised the Lord Jesus will raise me with Him and will set you side by side with me in His presence. All this then is done on account of you, in order that the more there are to participate in His grace the more thanksgiving may arise to the glory of God.

[16] Far then from giving up, I find that, in proportion as my physical powers fail, my spiritual energy is being renewed day by day. Our light and passing troubles earn for us a degree of glory that is eternal and utterly incomparable, so long as we fix our gaze on the invisible rather than on the visible, for the visible is merely temporary, but the invisible is eternal.

V

The Earthly and the Heavenly

I know that when the time comes for me to fold up this feeble tent and steal away I shall have a home with God, a house built without hands, eternal in Heaven. As things are, I often sigh and long to find myself under the protection of that heavenly roof, so that I may never be found without a covering. While we are in our present temporary abode we sigh under our burdens, not because we wish to dispense with all covering, but rather because we desire that we may be better housed, and that what is mortal may be absorbed into life. For such a change we have been prepared by God Himself who has given us a guarantee in His Spirit. And that gives one plenty of courage. I realize, too, that so long as I am alive in the body I am absent from the Lord. So my guide is faith, not physical sight. Courage spurs me to prefer absence from the body and presence with the Lord. In either case I make it a point of honour, whether present or absent, to be pleasing to Him. We must all appear one day before the bar of Christ. There every man will be judged according to what he has done in the body whether good or bad.

The Ministry of Reconciliation

[11] It is in the light of such fear of God that I make my own special appeal. My motive is open to God and I hope it will be clear to your conscience too. I am not going to begin defending myself all over again, but I want to give you some justification for your pride in me, so that you can produce it against those who take pride in superficialities rather than in the inner realities of the heart. If my enthusiasm makes me seem, as my critics say, 'a bit mad', it is for God's honour; if on the other hand I display any worldly wisdom, it is for your benefit. What drives me on is the love of Christ, for I consider that as One died for all, all are dead. But He died for all in order that those who are made alive should not live to themselves but to Him who died for them and rose again. So from now on I no longer recognize people by their physical attributes. Even if I had known Christ in the flesh, I should know Him in that way no longer. Similarly he who is in Christ is a new creation: the old has passed away; what is here now is new. But everything comes from God, who has reconciled us to Himself through Christ, and has committed to me the ministry of reconciliation. That ministry is based on the fact that God was in Christ reconciling the world to Himself, wiping out the debit balance of our transgressions and setting His reconciliation to the credit of our account.

The Envoy of Christ

[20] So I am an ambassador of Christ, and God appeals to you through me. On behalf of Christ I beg you make your peace with God. Christ who was innocent of sin He made to be sin on our behalf that in Him we might become the righteousness of God.

VI

As a fellow-worker with God I beg you not to receive the grace of God in vain. As God said,

> Good was the day you chose for your request,
> Salvation then I gave at your behest.

That good day, that day of salvation, is To-day.

[3] I am anxious not to put an obstacle in any man's path; so careful am I not to have my ministry discredited in other people's eyes. By every means I consolidate my position as a minister of God, although the effort has involved much suffering, affliction, trouble, sorrow, even beating and imprisonment. I have been mobbed and I have been overworked, with my strength reduced by sleeplessness and lack of food. Yet I have not failed in innocence, knowledge, patience, kindness, inspiration of the Holy Spirit, sincerity of love, truth in argument or power of God. I have dealt doughty blows for righteousness to right and left, and have remained indifferent to glory and shame, to renown and disrepute. I am an 'impostor' and yet genuine, 'unknown' and yet openly approved, 'defunct' yet very much alive, 'beaten' but not killed, 'gloomy' yet always cheerful, 'poverty-stricken' yet bringing riches to many, 'penniless' yet possessing everything.

You know, I am talking much too freely to you Corinthians, but my feelings carry me away. Certainly if there is any constraint in our mutual relations it is not on my side but on yours. 'Fair do's,' as the children say. You should let your feelings towards me carry you away too.

[Fragment of another Letter

[14] Don't get yourselves mixed up with unbelievers: there can be nothing in common between righteousness and lawlessness any more than between light and darkness. What agreement can there be between Christ and the Devil, or what part has the believer with the unbeliever? How does the temple of God

accord with idols? And we are the temple of the Living God, as He Himself has said:

> With them shall be my dwelling and my walk,
> And they shall be my people, I their God.
> Therefore depart, all ye that are not theirs,
> And keep yourselves removed. Thus saith the Lord,
> Touch not, my People, aught that is not clean
> And I will then receive you as my own,
> And be a Father to you, saith your God.
> While you shall sons and daughters be to me.

VII

Since then these promises are ours, let us cleanse ourselves, beloved, from every defilement of body and soul and make perfect our holiness in the fear of God.]

Paul's Appeal

[2] Give me a place in your affections. I have not wronged any of you, or corrupted you, or taken advantage of you. Nor am I criticizing you. I have said already that, come life, come death, you are firmly planted in my affections. I have great confidence in you and I am very proud of you. You are a great comfort to me, and even in the midst of all my troubles, the mere thought of you overwhelms me with happiness.

The Crisis settled

[5] When I went to Macedonia, I was very restless and found trouble everywhere. Everyone was quarrelling: my own mind was full of fears. But God who comforts the sorrowful comforted me by sending Titus to me. It was not only the comfort of his presence which was such a help to me, but the news of the support you had given him. He told me of your longing to see me, your sorrow at my misfortunes and your desire to help. All that filled me with joy. I know that my letter upset you, but I am not sorry for that. I was sorry; but now that I see the upset was soon

over, I am glad because you were stirred to repentance. You were upset in the way God wants us to be, and so you took no harm at my hands. Grief that submits itself to God brings repentance, and so results in a salvation which leaves no place for regret. But grief that ignores God ends in death. See what zeal this same godly grief has aroused in you, what anxiety to clear yourselves. You are indignant, alarmed, eager, determined, bursting to vindicate yourselves. In every respect you have shown yourselves to be blameless in this affair.

[12] When I wrote to you it was for the sake neither of the offender nor of the injured party, but simply to give you a chance of realizing before God the goodwill you bear me. The fact that you did do so was a great comfort to me. And in addition to this comfort for myself, I was overjoyed at the delight of Titus in the fact that you had all united to set his mind at rest. It showed that my pride in you was not misplaced, and as I have always been scrupulously truthful in speaking to you, so now my boasting about you in the presence of Titus has proved similarly true. His heart is full to overflowing every time he thinks of your submissiveness and of the respect and reverence with which you received him. So I am glad that in every way I can maintain my confidence in you.

VIII

Reasons for Urgency

Now I must tell you, brothers, about the wonderful opportunity God has given to the churches in Macedonia, and how they turned the trial of a great affliction into abundant joy, and dire poverty into the purest form of riches. I can affirm that up to the limit of their capacity and even beyond it they have spontaneously begged me with the utmost urgency to give them the privilege of contributing to the needs of our Christian brethren. They even surpassed my expectations, for they first of all surrendered themselves to the Lord and also to me (so far, of course, as is consistent with the will of God). That was what led me to summon Titus, the originator of this scheme, in order that he might complete it by extending the same privilege and oppor-

tunity to you. You already excel in so many respects, in faith, in
reason, in knowledge, in every kind of zeal and in love for me;
so now you must let us see how you can excel in this gracious act.

I am not laying upon you a command, but using the earnest
zeal of others as a means of testing the worth of your love for me.
You know what graciousness was shown by our Lord Jesus Christ,
how, although He was so rich, yet for your sakes He became
poor, in order that you might as a result of His poverty become
rich. I really think that as you were the first a year ago, not only
to start working this scheme, but actually to suggest it, now it
would be well for you to carry it through to a conclusion. In that
way you will show that as you had the readiness to propose it,
so you have also the courage to carry it out—as far, of course, as
you are able. So long as the willingness is there you will only be
expected to give in proportion to your means; you will not be
expected to give what you have not. There is no intention to let
other people off lightly by imposing a burden upon you, but
rather to put everyone on an equality. On the present occasion
your wealth will make up for their poverty, but on another
occasion their wealth will make up for your poverty. So everything is equalled out in the end. You remember the text: 'He
that had much had nothing over, and he that had little suffered
no lack.'

Commendation of Titus

[16] I am grateful to God for planting so deep an affection for
you in the heart of Titus. He did not come to you merely because
I sent him, but because he was sufficiently eager on his own
account. With him I sent the brother whose fame as an evangelist
is known to all the churches. He had also been chosen by the
churches to be my fellow-traveller for the purpose of administer-
ing this charity to the glory of God. That suited me, for I was
anxious to avoid the possibility of any suspicion arising out of the
management of this business. I want what we do to appear
praiseworthy not only to God but also to men. With them I sent
the brother whose keenness I have proved on many occasions,
and who is now keener than ever because of the confidence he
has in you. If then any question arises about Titus, he is my

colleague sharing my duty towards you; or if about the brothers, they are apostles of the churches, part of Christ's peculiar glory. Give them some proof then of your love for me, and afford them some justification of my pride in you for the benefit of the other churches.

IX

Confidence in a Liberal Response

But to get back to the question of this collection for the needy brethren. It is really superfluous for me to write about it. I know how keen you are. I remember too how I boasted of your eagerness to the Macedonians and told them that Achaia had made its preparations a year ago. Your keenness stirred up a great number of them. I am sending the brethren to make sure that my boasting about you in this instance should not be proved idle. As I have said you are ready, I should be put out of countenance if any Macedonians happened to come with me and found you not ready—and you would share my embarrassment. So I considered it necessary to summon the brethren and send them in advance to collect your promised contribution beforehand, so that it may be seen to be a voluntary contribution and not something wrung out of you. Remember this, that the man who sows little reaps little, but he who sows generously reaps a generous harvest. Let each of you make up his own mind, not grudgingly or out of necessity. God loves a cheerful giver And He is able to provide amply for your every need, so that you may not only have enough to satisfy every possible want of your own, but also may have plenty for any kind act to another. That's what the Scripture says:

To the poor far and wide He has opened His hand,
His goodness shall never depart from the land.

He who provides seed for sowing and bread for eating will provide plenty of seed for you and give you more and more opportunities to let it grow into works of charity. You will be richly endowed for every sort of generosity, and thus I shall be your agent in bringing much gratitude to God. For the administration of this charity will not only supply the wants of our poorer members, it will also produce a great wave of thanksgiving to God. In recognition of this service that you are rendering men will give glory to God, because they will be convinced that you practise the gospel of Christ you profess and are whole-hearted in the good-fellowship you show to them and to everyone. They will pray for you and have all the greater regard for you on account of the very special grace of God displayed in your case.

Thanks be to God for His indescribable goodness.

[*The remainder of this epistle down to XIII* 10 *forms part of the* '*severe*' *letter, that is, the third of the four letters mentioned in the Preface.*]

X

The First Charge . . . Feebleness

Now I, Paul, myself beseech you by the gentleness and considerateness of Christ, listen to me. You say that I was humble enough when I was with you, but that now I am away I am putting on airs. I hope that when I am with you I shall not have to display that authority which I expect to show in the case of some who have been arguing that my manner of life is sensual. If that is the way I live, it is not the way I fight. The weapons I use are not sensual weapons, but divinely tempered to demolish whole forts and bastions of argumentation and strong points erected against the knowledge of God. I take captive every thought and make it obedient to Christ, and I am ready to punish any insubordination, once I have you properly under control.

[7] Don't ignore this obvious fact—that if one is ever justified in believing that he belongs to Christ, then I most certainly have as strong a claim as any. If I boast a little too much about my authority (which the Lord gave me to help you and not to thwart you), I shall not be discredited as if I were just trying to overawe you with a letter. 'His letters,' somebody says, 'are solemn and portentous, but when he comes along you will see what a weakling he is, and his speechifying amounts to nothing.' Well, let

that person take note of this, that what I appear to be in the phraseology of my letters, precisely that will I be in actual deed when I arrive among you.

[12] I shall not venture to include myself or to compare myself with certain individuals who are busy establishing their own reputation. They make the mistake of measuring and comparing themselves by their common standard. I am not given to immeasurable pretensions; I confine myself strictly within the limits set me by God. But those limits do include you.

[14] I am not overreaching myself as if you were outside the limits of my authority, for I was the first to bring you the gospel of Christ. I am not making unlimited claims on the basis of someone else's labours, although I am confident that your faith will increase and grow after the pattern I set you until it overflows and allows me to extend my preaching beyond your boundaries. I do not want to take credit for work put ready to my hand in someone else's territory. 'Let him who boasts, boast in the Lord.' A man's worth is not estimated at his own valuation, but at the Lord's.

XI

Second Charge . . . Refusal of Hospitality

I must apologize for talking in this somewhat undignified fashion. But I hope you will put up with it, for I am consumed with a sort of supernatural love on your behalf. I betrothed you to one Lord and Master, Christ, like a virgin bride to her husband. But I am afraid that, as Eve was deceived by the serpent's wiles, so your minds may lose something of their original simplicity and purity towards Christ. When a new-comer preaches a different Jesus from the one I preached, and when you receive a different Spirit from the one you have received, or a different gospel from the one you have already heard, how easily you put up with the change. Yet I do not think I am in the least inferior to those extraordinary 'apostles'. If I am 'not much of a speaker', I have at least a fair amount of knowledge, and I always managed to convey my full meaning to you.

[7] Did I make a mistake in trying to exalt you to the heights by rating myself so low, and in preaching the gospel to you without making any charge for my services? During my ministry to you I kept myself by taking money from other churches. If I was in actual want while I was with you, I never became an encumbrance on any of you, for the brothers who came from Macedonia satisfied all my needs. In every respect I carefully guarded against becoming a burden to you, and I shall continue to do so. I am speaking the precise truth when I say that so far as I am concerned I shall not allow the boast I made to be proved false in any part of Achaia. Why? Because I don't love you? God knows I do. But the course upon which I set, and upon which I shall continue, is intended to expose the pretensions of those who deliberately give themselves airs, and to show that all their boasting does not make them any better than myself. They are false apostles, impostors masquerading as Apostles of Christ. We need not be surprised at that, for even Satan masquerades as an angel of light. No wonder then if his servants disguise themselves as servants of righteousness. But their end will be a fitting climax to their deeds.

Third Charge . . . Defective Authority

[16] Again I ask, don't let anyone think me foolish. But if any of you do, then bear with my folly a moment so that I may make one further boast. What I am about to say I do not profess to say by divine inspiration, but out of that same foolish and yet confident boasting. If others make a practice of this paltry self-glorification, I must do the same. You are so wise yourselves that you can easily put up with a little folly in others. You even put up with those who tyrannize over you, impose upon you, trap you, override you, slap your face. What a shame that I could not do anything like that. But if any of them have claims to put forward (now I *am* talking foolishly) I can do it too. Are they Hebrews? So am I. Israelites? So am I. Descendants of Abraham? So am I. Christian ministers? (Here's a pitch of folly) I am more. Overwhelmed with toil and imprisonment, cruelly flogged, often in danger of death. Five times I have received the maximum punishment of thirty-nine lashes from the

Jews; three times a Roman beating; once I was stoned; three times shipwrecked; twenty-four hours in the water; on constant journeys with danger from floods and robbers, from my own countrymen as well as foreigners, and in perils of city, sea and desert, as well as treachery on the part of fellow-believers; in toil and trouble, in much want of sleep, in hunger and thirst, in frequent fasts, frozen from want of clothing. In addition to all these extra worries there is that which is my daily portion, the supervision of all the churches. Who shows weakness without me being affected by it? Who stumbles without me being consumed with anxiety? If I must boast, I will boast of my disabilities. The God and Father of our Lord Jesus Christ, who is blessed for ever, is witness to the truth of what I say. Why, actually at Damascus the Governor appointed by King Aretas kept a close watch throughout the city in the hope of apprehending me, but I was lowered through a loophole down the wall in a basket and so escaped his clutches.

XII

Fourth Charge . . . Lack of Spiritual Experience

But if I have to go on boasting, useless as it is, I will come to visions and revelations of the Lord. I know a man in Christ who fourteen years ago was rapt into the third heaven. Whether it was a physical or a spiritual experience I don't know, God alone knows. I only know that the man was caught up into paradise and heard things too sacred for repetition, and not to be repeated. I say again that whether this was a physical or a spiritual experience I don't know, only God knows. Of such an experience I will boast, but I will not boast about myself—except in respect of my disabilities. (Though if I did make up my mind to boast, I should not convict myself of folly, for I should be speaking the truth. However, I will refrain, for I don't want anyone to think more highly of me than he is justified in doing from what he himself sees and hears.) Astounding revelations were granted me, but to prevent me from falling into conceit on that account there was given me also a grave physical weakness, Satan's own agent sent to torment me and to prevent me from falling into self-conceit. Three times I called for the Lord's help in this matter, praying that He would release me from this trouble. But He told me, 'My help is all you need, for in your weakness my strength is able to do its proper work.' That is why I much prefer to boast of my weakness, for it is then that the strength of Christ rests upon me. So I rejoice in periods of weakness, in insults, in hard times, in persecutions, in calamities for the sake of Christ. For when I am weak, then am I strong.

[11] Now I am being foolish. But it is your fault; you ought yourselves to have recognized me for what I am, and spared me the necessity of stating my own case. Even if I am nothing, I am not at all inferior to your super-apostles. I have displayed all the signs of apostleship among you by all that I have endured, and by the performance of miracles, wonders and works of power. Did I treat you as in any way inferior to the other churches, except in this one thing—that I would not make myself a burden to you? Please forgive me for slighting you so.

Fifth Charge . . . The Question of Support

[14] Anyhow, this is the third time I have made arrangements to visit you, and I will *not* be a burden to you. I don't want your gifts, but you. It is not the children's duty to lay by for the parents, but the parents' for the children. And I will gladly spend and be spent for the good of your souls. Are you going to take advantage of my special affection for you and show me proportionately less in return?

[16] 'All right,' you say, 'we will let that pass. You never were a burden to us. No, you were too clever for that. You got your hold on us by a trick.' How did I do that? Did I batten on you through any of the men I sent you? I summoned Titus and sent our brother with him. Did Titus batten on you? Is not his conduct ruled by the same Spirit as mine? Don't we tread in the same footprints?

[19] I hope you don't think that in all this I am trying to build up some sort of defence for myself. I am speaking solemnly as in the presence of God and in union with Christ; and, beloved, I

am doing it all for the sake of your own spiritual training. I have a sort of fear that when I come I shall be disappointed in you and you in me. I am afraid there may be quarrels, party strife, angry feelings, rivalries, libels, slanders, insubordination, rebellion. And I am afraid that when I come again God may let me be humiliated in respect of you, and I shall have cause to grieve for many who have previously sinned and have not repented of their filthy, immoral, licentious behaviour.

XIII

Warning and Appeal

This then will be my third visit to you. 'Every proof must be based on the evidence of two or three witnesses.' I warned you when I was with you the second time, and do so now again before I meet you, both the early offenders and all the rest, that when I do come again I shall show you no leniency. That will prove to you that Christ speaks through me, for while He will show no weakness towards you, He will certainly show strength in me. What if He did reveal a sort of weakness in being crucified? In His new life He now reveals the power of God. I share His weakness, but I shall also share His life in the power of God towards you.

[5] Test yourselves to see whether you are in the faith; try yourselves out. Don't you recognize that Jesus Christ is in you? That is, if you have not been rejected. I trust you realize that I at any rate have not been rejected. I pray God you will not take the wrong line, not because I want to be proved in the right, but that you may take the proper course even if I am proved in the wrong. In any case, I cannot fight against the truth, but only in support of it. If I should happen to show weakness while you showed strength, I should be quite happy about it. I pray only for your perfection.

[10] I am writing in this fashion while I am still away from you, in order that when I am with you I shall not have to deal summarily with you. The authority given me by Christ would

6

warrant me in so doing, but, after all, that authority was given me for your edification and not for your destruction.

Conclusion

[11]   Well, brothers, I must say good-bye. Restore one another, comfort one another, find a common purpose, cultivate peace, and the God of love and of peace will be with you. When you meet, embrace one another reverently. All the church people here send their greetings.

[13]   May the grace of the Lord Jesus Christ and the love of God and the comradeship of the Holy Spirit be with you all.

Romans

S. Paul had intended to extend his Third Missionary Journey to Rome. But when the collection for the Jerusalem Christians proved so great a success, he judged it right to shorten his itinerary and to act as his own agent in the conveyance of the alms. Such a gesture would show his essential good-will to the Jewish Christians and help to remove any trace of ill-feeling. He therefore wrote from Corinth to explain to the Christians in Rome his present inability to visit them and to promise to do so when he should fulfil his ambition to make a journey to Spain.

He takes the opportunity to set out on a fuller scale than hitherto his theological position. As the Roman Church consisted of both Jews and Gentiles, it was natural that he should deal with the vexed question of the relation between the Law and the Gospel. If God had always intended to save the world by the death and resurrection of Jesus Christ, why had there ever been a Law of Moses? And if people are saved by simple faith in Christ, are they not subject to any law at all?

These questions have important bearings in both the historical and the psychological fields, and S. Paul deals with both alike. He justifies God's ways in history by showing that the Law was a valuable preparation for the Gospel. And psychologically, he affirms, only those who are 'in Christ' are capable of rising to the full height of the moral law.

This epistle is thus of outstanding importance, because it gives both S. Paul's theology of salvation and his philosophy of history.

S. Paul's Letter To The Romans

I

My dear Fellow-Christians,

A humble slave of Christ ventures to address himself to the church in Rome. Yet the slave is an Apostle, separated from the rest of mankind by Divine calling to preach the Gospel of God. That 'Good News' God announced long ago through His prophets who were responsible for the Holy Scriptures concerning His Son. By genealogy, of course, Jesus belonged to the line of David, but He was shewn to be also Son of God in unmistakable fashion when the Holy Spirit raised Him from the dead. This Jesus we recognize as our Lord, and it is through Him that I have received my commission as Apostle. My business is to win converts, who shall be faithful and loyal to Him, from among all non-Jews everywhere. In this number you yourselves are already reckoned, for you too have been called by Jesus Christ. To all of you, God's own beloved, I send greeting, and I pray that you may receive the gift of grace and peace from God our Father and the Lord Jesus Christ.

A Word of Thanks

[8] At the outset let me express my thankfulness on account of you all, for your loyalty has been proclaimed through the whole world. God knows (and you will forgive me for saying this, for I have no reserves where my service of God and the gospel of His Son is concerned) that I never cease to mention you in my prayers. And I always ask that if it be His will I may be given a favourable opportunity to visit you. I am longing to see you in order that I may hand on to you some spiritual gifts to make you still stronger Christians and that I myself may be comforted by our common loyalty and mutual friendship. I should like you to know, my brothers, that I have often planned to come to you but have been prevented up till now. I did so want to win some converts in Rome as well as in the rest of the Pagan world.

[14] I owe a duty to Greek-speaking people as well as to Barbarians, to the cultured as well as to the uncouth. That explains my zeal to preach the Gospel to you in Rome. I am not ashamed to proclaim the Gospel. It represents the power of God to save *everyone who believes*, the Jew first and then the Greek. In it the justice of God's way is made clear in proportion to our belief. That is why the Scripture says, 'Belief is the good man's very breath of life.'

Judgment on the Gentile World

[18] God has made quite clear His anger against all the iniquity of those Pagans who by their wickedness hinder the spread of truth. What may be known of God should have been obvious to them, for He has made it plain. Actually ever since the world began the invisible character of God, His eternal power and divine being, has been discernible in His handiwork. So the Pagans have no excuse. For though they recognized God, they did not worship Him as God or give Him thanks, but they wasted their time in arguments, and their minds became clouded by the darkness of ignorance. While they claimed to be wise they became really stupid, and they exchanged the glory of the immortal God for effigies of mortal men and even birds and beasts and reptiles.

[24] So God let them fall into vile passions and utter filthiness such as debased their bodies. For they turned divine truth into falsehood, worshipping and serving created things instead of the Creator (Blessed be He for ever).

[26] For this reason has God given them up to dishonourable passions. Their very women changed natural use into unnatural vice. Similarly the men, avoiding natural intercourse with the opposite sex, were consumed with homosexual lusts, and suffered in their own persons the inevitable consequences of their depravity.

[28] Thus as they closed their minds to all knowledge of God He gave them up to abandoned impulses. They broke all laws of conduct; they practised every kind of wickedness—lust, passion,

vice. In consequence they are eaten up with jealousy, parricide, quarrelsomeness, deceit, degeneracy. They are slanderers, gossipers, impious, insolent, over-bearing, swaggering, inventors of new vices, home-breakers, without consistency, without compassion, without mercy. They know perfectly well God's judgement—that they who practise such things shall be punished with death. Yet they not only do these things themselves, but entice others to do them.

II

Judgment on Jews

However it is no part of our business to be censorious, for in unduly criticizing our neighbours we condemn ourselves. Only too often the critic is guilty of the same faults. But we know that God's judgment against such practices is inevitable. Can we, if we indulge in the same conduct while criticizing others, imagine that we shall escape God's judgment? Or are we so contemptuous of His great goodness and patience and forbearance as not to realize that His kindness is intended to lead us to repentance? Through stubbornness and impenitence we shall surely lay up for ourselves wrath against the day when the judgment of God shall be revealed in all its just severity. For 'He shall reward each man according to his deeds'. Therefore to those who have by good works patiently pursued glory and honour and immortality shall be granted life eternal. But to those who out of contrariness disobey the truth and follow wickedness there will be awarded only anger and wrath. It will mean affliction and calamity for every person who works evil, Jews first and then Greeks. But it will mean glory and honour and peace to everyone who does good, Jews first and then Greeks. For God has no favourites.

[12] This means that the Jews' standard of attainment will be judged in accordance with the provisions of the Mosaic Law, and that the Pagans' standard will be judged under natural law. It is not *knowledge* of the Mosaic Law that justifies a man in the sight of God, but the keeping of it. When Pagans, who are outside the Law, do naturally what the Law demands they obviously reveal the existence of a Natural Law of their own. You can see it

written, as it were, in their hearts, for they obey the dictates of their conscience, and their conduct is either approved or condemned by their own moral convictions. That will be made plain, if my version of the Gospel is true, in the day when God judges the secrets of men's hearts through Christ Jesus.

[17] But suppose you are correctly styled a 'Jew', and take your stand on the Law, and boast that God is on your side and that you know His will; and suppose that, having been taught out of the Law, you are capable of some hair-splitting in regard to it, and consider yourself a guide of the blind, a light to those darkened by ignorance, an instructor of the foolish, a teacher of the kindergarten, and believe that in the Law you have the compendium of all true knowledge. Well, if you teach others, can't you teach yourself? If you repeat the commandment not to steal, do you steal? The man who forbids adultery ought not to commit it himself. The man who abominates idols should not rob heathen shrines and so make an idol of covetousness. The man who takes pride in being under the Law should not transgress the Law and so dishonour God. Remember what the Scriptures say, 'It is on account of such as you that the Name of God is held in dishonour among the Pagans'.

[25] Circumcision is an advantage if you keep the Law, but if you don't keep the Law your circumcision is a positive disadvantage. Conversely, if a man keeps the moral elements of the Law without circumcision, surely the mere lack of circumcision will not be counted against him. Indeed, such a Nature's Gentleman will be in a position to judge you, who in spite of your circumcision are really a law-breaker. It is not the outward sign that makes the Jew: no mere operation on the flesh can do that. He is a Jew who is one inwardly, circumcised in the heart, not physically but spiritually. He it is who earns praise, not from men but from God.

III

Sin is Universal

What advantage then is there in being a Jew, and what good is there in being circumcised? A great deal. First it was the

Jews whom God made the instruments of His revelation. It is
true that some of them lost their faith, but their unbelief cannot
cancel the loyalty of God. Indeed no! God would still be true
though every man were proved a liar. Remember the lines:

> Of all God says to man
> The truth can soon be taught,
> And who dares question Him
> Is quick to silence brought.

Does this mean that God's righteousness can only be brought
out by our wickedness? 'Excuse the anthropomorphism', you
may say, 'but isn't He Himself wicked in shewing anger?' Certainly not. How in that case could God judge the world? But
then, you will perhaps argue, if God's truth needs my lie to throw
it into relief, why am I condemned as a sinner? That is getting
near the blasphemous position that good depends upon evil.
There are some indeed who actually accuse me of saying that
we must do evil in order that good may result. That is nonsense.

[9] But to get back to our point. Are we Jews likely to be
specially favoured because we enjoy the advantage of the Law?
By no means. I have already placed all Jews and Pagans alike
under one general accusation of sinfulness. You remember the
words:

> No just man now remains
> Keen insight none displays
> The seekers after God
> Have strayed down evil ways.
>
> Foul-mouthed as open graves
> Their tongues spit forth deceit;
> Behind the fangs of asps
> Their poison-ducts retreat.
>
> To murder they have run,
> In sorrow's path they trod;
> Far from the ways of peace,
> Their eyes are blind to God.

[19]   We know that whatever the Law says to those who are
bound by it, it says in order to silence every objection and to
make the whole world amenable to God.   The fact is that absolutely no one can be completely vindicated under the terms of the
Law.   It was indeed through the Law that man gained the
knowledge of Sin.

Only one Means of Escape

[21]   But now the righteousness of God has been manifested
quite apart from the Law.   As we have shewn on the evidence of
both the Law and the Prophets the righteousness of God has been
made available through faith in Jesus Christ for all who believe.
There is therefore no distinction.   All alike have sinned and fallen
short of the Divine glory, but all alike may be freely acquitted
through God's generosity, which has been made possible as a
result of the redemption effected by Christ Jesus.   He was divinely
appointed to make up for our misdeeds and to reconcile us to
God.   That reconciliation we can appropriate for ourselves by
trusting to the efficacy of His self-sacrifice.   Thus God makes clear
that He does no violence to His own justice in passing over the
old sins and forbearing to punish them.   His essential justice He
has made clear to us in this generation.   And He not only shows
Himself just but He justifies also those who by faith identify themselves with Jesus.

[27]   There is thus no room for anyone to boast.   The fact that
in the last resort we must rely, not on any success in observing
the Law, but simply on faith, makes boasting impossible.   I have
shewn that a man is vindicated before God not by carrying out
the commands of the Law but by faith.   That after all is the only
possible way, for God is not the God of the Jews only, nor of the
Pagans only, but of both.   There is only one God, and He will
vindicate the circumcised on the score of their faith and the uncircumcised for precisely the same reason.

[31]   Do we then nullify the Law by this faith?   Certainly not.
We actually establish the very reason for its existence.

IV

The Example of the Patriarch Abraham

Let us take the crucial instance of our forefather Abraham. What was it that happened in his case? If he had been reckoned an innocent man as the result of his own efforts, he might have felt a natural pride. But that was not enough for God. You remember what the Scripture says: 'Abraham had faith in God, and it was on that account that he was reckoned righteous.' You see the difference. If a man *works*, his wages are handed over to him not as a free gift but as a due. On the other hand if a man makes no effort of his own but simply puts his trust in Him who justifies sinners, then there is nothing but his faith that can be reckoned to him for righteousness. That is what the Psalmist means when he speaks of the blessedness of the man to whom God attributes righteousness apart from any works of his own:

> Blessed is the man
>> For whom atonement's made
>> Whose sin is all forgiven
>> And no fresh charge is laid.
> Blessed is that man.

[9] You may ask whether this blessedness is confined to the Circumcision or whether it is granted to the uncircumcised as well. The answer can be found in the text I have just quoted: 'Abraham had faith in God and it was on that account that he was reckoned righteous.' The point is that faith was accredited to him not after, but before, he was circumcised. That operation took place later and was performed as a kind of sign or seal of the faith that he had already shewn in his uncircumcised condition. By this fact he became the progenitor both of all the uncircumcised who have faith and whose faith is counted to them for righteousness, and also of all the circumcised who do not rely upon circumcision for their salvation, but show evidence of that faith which was characteristic of the still-uncircumcised Abraham.

[13] The promise that they should inherit the earth was not made to Abraham and his descendants on account of their

obedience to the Law, but because of the righteousness that springs from faith. Obviously if they were made heirs because of the Law, their faith was of no value and the promise lapsed. As a matter of fact the Law establishes nothing except penalties. But if there is no Law there are no breaches to be penalized. So there is no question of rewards or penalties, but the assured promise rests on one and the same condition for all Abraham's descendants alike, both those who practise the Law and those who do not. Thus Abraham is the progenitor of us all alike, as the Scripture itself points out: 'I have made thee a father of many nations.'

[17] The reason for this is that he staked everything on the existence of a God who makes the dead live and calls into being things that had no previous existence. To that faith he adhered, hoping against hope. And this belief was justified, for he did indeed become the father of many nations just as he was told, 'You shall have many descendants.' His faith must have been truly extraordinary, for he was a hundred years old and he knew that he and his wife were both impotent. But he did not in the least degree doubt the promise God had made. Through this trustfulness he regained his virility. He acknowledged the supreme power of God and was convinced that He was strong enough to do what He had promised. It was this attitude of mind that was 'reckoned to him for righteousness'.

[23] That last phrase does not apply to him only but to all of us who believe that God raised up Jesus our Lord from the dead. Our trust in Him is reckoned to us for righteousness. For Jesus who was delivered up to death on account of our transgressions was actually raised again for our acquittal.

V

The Glorious Confidence of the Redeemed

Since then we have been acquitted on the score of faith, let us be at peace with God through our Lord Jesus Christ. Through Him we have been introduced by faith to the state of grace wherein we now stand, and we take pride in our expectation that we shall share in an ultimate manifestation of God's glory. Not only so, but we also take pride in our afflictions. For we know that these are necessary for the training of our character. Affliction produces endurance, and endurance produces reliability, and reliability produces confidence. And our confidence, we are certain, will not be disappointed, for the love of God is poured into our hearts through the gift of the Holy Spirit. This is shewn most signally in the fact that, in the very midst of our weakness, at the psychological moment Christ died for the unrighteous. It is not often that one can be found to sacrifice his life even for a good man. But to save a good man perhaps one here and there will be ready to die. The special quality of God's love for us is seen in the fact that it was while we were still sinners that Christ died for us.

[9] Now that we have been thus acquitted, we have a stronger guarantee than ever that through His self-sacrifice we shall be saved from the final Wrath. For if while we were sinners we were reconciled to God through the death of His Son much more when we are already reconciled shall we be saved by His life. And this is the cause of our great pride in God through our Lord Jesus Christ, through whom we have now been granted reconciliation.

[12] Thus we see that, as by one man sin entered the world and the consequence of sin was death, so death came upon all men because all inherited his sinful nature. For sin was in the world already before the introduction of the Law. However, until there was a Law no one could be charged with sin. Nevertheless everyone was subject to death from the time of Adam until Moses, even if they had not followed the sinful example of Adam.

[15] The first Man, Adam, was a type of the Man-who-was-to-come, or the Reedemer. But we must certainly place God's free gift in a different category from Adam's transgression. And that for two reasons. First, if the transgression of the Original Man brought about the death of many, much rather will the Grace of God, manifested in the gift of the Unique Person, Jesus Christ, result in blessing for the many. And in a second way the gift is different: it does not come as the result of a single sin (in that case judgment brought condemnation), but in response to a whole

multitude of transgressions in order to ensure pardon. If then by one man's transgression all became the subjects of death, much more shall those who receive the bounty of God and the gift of righteousness through the Unique Person Jesus Christ become the lords of life.

[18] Thus as through the transgression of one all were condemned to death, so through the restitution of One all were set free for righteous living. And as through one man's disobedience the many were reckoned sinners, so by One's obedience the many were reckoned righteous.

[20] The role played by the Law was to underline the offence, but where sin was emphasized grace was bestowed the more freely. So just when sin and death seemed to be the reigning powers grace took possession of the throne, and that by means of a righteousness that opened the way to eternal life through Jesus Christ our Lord.

VI

In Christ we have passed already from Sinful Death to Holy Life

Well then, how shall we conclude the argument? Shall we say that we ought to keep on sinning so that there may be more and more grace? Certainly not. If we have died to sin, we can't continue to practise sin. Isn't that the meaning of Baptism? When we were baptized we shared in the death of Christ. When the water flowed over us it was as if we were in the grave with Him. But as Christ was raised from the dead by the power of the Father's glory, so we rise from the watery grave and move freely in a new life. Or to change the metaphor, if by this sharing of His death we were 'grafted into Him', much more by sharing His resurrection shall we grow into Him. We must recognize that our old nature was crucified with Him in order that our body might be freed from all sinful tendencies, and that we should no longer be the slaves of sin. For of course every man who has died has paid the penalty of sin.

[8] If we have shared Christ's death we believe that we shall also share His life. For we know that since Christ has been raised

from the dead He will not die again. He is no longer subject to
death. His death paid the penalty for sin once and for all. His
life is henceforth lived without limit for God. In the same way
we must account ourselves as truly dead to sin but alive to God
in Christ Jesus.

[12] Do not let sin have control in your mortal bodies or you
will become slaves to its lusts. And do not surrender your lives
to sin as if they were the agents of wickedness, but surrender
yourselves to God as is proper for those who are alive from the
dead. Hand over your lives to God as agents of righteousness.
Sin must not be your Lord. You are not subject to the Law but
to Grace.

[15] Well then, shall we feel ourselves free to sin because we
are not under the Law but under Grace? By no means. Don't
you realize that if you make yourself someone's slave, you become
his altogether? So you can be either slaves of sin right up to the
inevitable consequence of death, or you can be slaves of obedience
with its equally inevitable result in righteousness. But I am
devoutly thankful that whereas you were once the slaves of sin,
you have now given your wholehearted obedience to the teaching
that you received. So now that you have been emancipated from
sin you have become slaves of righteousness. Forgive me if I talk
in blunt language in order to bring my point home. You did once
hand over your bodies as slaves to immorality and to one piece
of lawlessness after another. In the same way you have now
handed over your bodies as slaves to a morality which culminates
in holiness.

[20] When you were the slaves of sin you enjoyed complete
freedom in respect of moral effort. But what good did you get
out of that? Nowadays you are thoroughly ashamed of such a
past. On the other hand now that you have been set free from
sin and become enslaved to God you find a real joy in holiness of
life. And the end of that state is life eternal. For the wage earned
by sin is death, but the free gift of God is eternal life in Christ
Jesus our Lord.

VII

Union with Christ frees us from the Law

You know, my brethren (I am speaking to those who are familiar with the Law), that a man is subject to the Law as long as life lasts. It is like marriage. A married woman is bound by law to her husband as long as he is living. But if the man dies she is free from marriage bonds. So long as her husband is alive she is deemed an adulteress if she has carnal intercourse with another man. But if the husband is dead she is free from his right over her and is no adulteress if she give herself in marriage to another.

[4] In the same way, my brethren, our obligations to the Law have been brought to an end by death; so that we may now be given to Another, even to Him who was raised from the dead, in order that we may bear fruit to God. When we were under the dominion of our lower nature the passions of sin awakened by the Law so wrought in our bodies that we bore fruit to Death. But now we have been set free from the Law; we have died to that which held us down; we are engaged in the new free-service of the spirit and not in the old slavery of the letter.

The Function of the Law to reveal the Heinousness of Sin

[7] Where is all this leading us? To the conclusion that the Law itself is sin? Certainly not. All the same I should not have known sin except for the Law. I should not have known for instance that there was such a thing as inordinate desire unless the Law had said 'Thou shalt not covet'. By the very prohibition the Law reinforced my sinful nature and stirred up in me all kinds of feverish lust. Apart from the Law sin is dormant (for if no commandment has been issued you have committed no offence). And I lived at one time without reference to the Law, but there came a commandment and sin leapt to life. But that involved death for me. The Law that was intended for life was found in my case to lead to death. For sin, receiving its impetus from the commandment, entrapped me, and then through the penalty attached to breach of the commandment slew me. By such means

is the purity of the Law maintained, and the regulations shewn to be holy, righteous and good.

[13] Is it then correct to say that something in itself good was responsible for my moral death? No! But sin, in order that it might be seen in its true colours, was allowed to use something inherently good to do me to death. It is thus by reason of the commandment that sin is recognized as being exceedingly sinful.

[14] The fact is that, whereas the Law is spiritual, I am carnal, enslaved by sin. I don't even understand my own actions. For it is not the things I should like to do that I actually do, but the things that I hate myself for doing. But if I don't like the things that I actually do, then tacitly at least I agree that the Law is right. However, it is not really I who do these things, but sin, which has taken possession of me.

[18] I know that in me, that is in my carnal nature, there remains nothing good. I still have power to wish, but not to accomplish, what is good. So far am I from doing the good I want to do, that I actually practise the evil that I hate. But if I fail to do what I really wish, it is obvious that it is no longer my true self that is responsible for the act but sin that has taken possession of me.

[21] I find then this rule in operation: that whenever I want to do good evil is triumphant. As far as my intentions are concerned I gladly accept the Law of God; but in my body I see a different law at work, struggling against the law of my mind and putting me in gondage to the law of sin which is proper to my lower nature. So in my mind I am subject to the law of God but in my flesh to the law of sin. Vile wretch that I am, who will deliver me from this death-infected body? I offer my thanks to God. He will do it through Christ Jesus our Lord.

VIII

Our Ultimate Glory is Secure

For those who are in Christ there is no condemnation. The law of the life-giving Spirit in Christ Jesus has set you free from the law of sin and death. What the Mosaic Law could not do owing to the frailty of the flesh, namely make men righteous, God has done in another way. He has sent His own Son in the guise of sinful flesh to deal with sin, and has condemned sin in the flesh.

[4] His purpose was to provide that the obligations of the Law might be fulfilled by us who enjoy our position as heirs through a spiritual rather than a fleshy relation. For those who emphasize the flesh think carnal thoughts, but those who are guided by the Spirit are spiritually minded. Carnal thoughts bring death, but to be spiritually minded is life and peace. The mind of the flesh (if I may venture to use such an expression) is at enmity with God, for it does not obey the law of God, and indeed it cannot do so. Those who are fleshly minded cannot please God.

[9] You however are not fleshly minded, if the Spirit of God dwells in you, but spiritually minded. Of course if we do not possess the Spirit of Christ we do not belong to Him. If on the other hand Christ is in you the flesh may be dead by reason of sin, but the spirit is alive by reason of righteousness. And is it not obvious that, if the Spirit of Him who raised up Jesus from the dead is in you, He will be able also to vivify even your mortal bodies?

[12] So, my brothers, we are under an obligation—but not to the flesh to live in accordance with its desires. If you live that way, death will be your portion. But if through the Spirit you die to the impulses of the body, you will live. For those who follow the guidance of the Spirit are indeed the Sons of God.

[15] The spirit you received was not a slavish spirit so that you should again fall into a condition of terror, but you received the filial spirit which enables us to address God confidently as Father. The Holy Spirit reinforces the dim consciousness of our own spirit that we are children of God. But if we are His children it follows that we are also His heirs. Thus we become joint heirs with Christ, sharing not only His sufferings, but also His legacy of eternal glory.

[18] I calculate that the sufferings of our present condition are infinitesimal compared with the glory that shall one day be ours. The whole created universe looks forward with eagerness to the revelation of that glory, to the moment when the sons of God

will be made known. For the physical world was made subject to frustration, not by its own desire, but by the will of the Creator, who in making it so, gave it a hope that it might one day be delivered from its bondage to corruption and made to share the glorious liberty of the children of God. We know that the created universe has been travailing in the pangs of a new birth right up to this present moment. In that travail we ourselves are included, even we who already feel within us the stirring of a new spiritual life, as we wait for our public recognition as sons, which will include our deliverance from the limitations of the body.

[24] Thus we are saved by hope. But hope that is fulfilled is no longer hope. It is the very essence of hope not to be fulfilled in the present. If you see your wish already granted, what is the point in still hoping for it? But if we hope for something not yet realized, we summon up our patience to wait for it.

[26] That is how the Spirit fortifies our weakness. We do not even know precisely what we ought to pray for. But the Spirit Himself comes to our assistance with inarticulate groanings. And He who searches our hearts knows what is the intention of the Spirit, namely to intercede in accordance with God's will on behalf of the Church.

[28] We know that everything contributes to the ultimate good of those who love God, of those, that is, who are chosen out from the rest of mankind in accordance with His plan. For He had certain people in mind from the beginning, and those He set apart beforehand to share the character of His Son, that the Son might be, as it were, the eldest among a whole family of brothers. And those whom He had set apart from the beginning, He actually called, and those whom He called He acquitted at the bar of Divine justice; and those He acquitted He also made to share His glory.

[31] To all this there is a corollary. If God is for us, who or what can possibly be against us? Surely He who did not spare His own Son but delivered Him up for us all, will together with this greatest of gifts grant us every other conceivable good. Who after that can bring any charge against those whom God has chosen? If God acquits, who will condemn? Certainly not

Christ Jesus, for He is the one who died, or rather was raised, for our sake, and was exalted to the right hand of God, where He now lives to make intercession on our behalf. What then can cut us off from the love of Christ? Can any affliction or catastrophe, such as persecution, or deprivation of food and clothing, or physical danger, or actual execution? We may now be sharing the fate of those of whom it is written:

> For Thy sake we suffer perpetual martyrdom,
> We are reckoned as sheep for the butcher.

But in spite of all we are winning an overwhelming victory through Him who gave us His love. I am absolutely confident that neither death, nor life, nor angels, nor demonic powers, nor present sufferings, nor future fate, nor dimensions in space, nor any created thing whatsoever can separate us from that love of God which has been manifested in Christ Jesus our Lord.

IX

God is not unjust in rejecting the Jews

I am speaking the simple truth and not some conventional hypocrisy when I say that I am suffering such continuous anguish of heart for those who by race are my own flesh and blood that I could wish myself damned for their sakes. They are Israelites. That means that they have inherited the adoption, the glory, the covenants, the Law, the worship—in fact all the revealed promises of God. To them also belong the Patriarchs, and of their blood sprang the Messiah (Blessed be His Divine Name above all for ever. Amen).

[6] It is not possible that the word of God should not come true. If He has seemed to reject Israel, we must remember that the true Israel is not necessarily to be identified with the people of Jewish blood. Not all those who are descended from Abraham are 'children of Abraham'. Indeed, the Scripture itself draws a distinction, for it says 'From Isaac shall your descent be reckoned'. That means that it is not the descendants by blood who are the Children of God, but that only those belong to the true line who

were born according to the supernatural promise. That was the
promise made to Sarah when she was past the proper age for
child-bearing: 'In due course I will come and Sarah shall have
a son.'

[10] That son was our Patriarch Isaac. And in the next generation he himself had a son by his wife Rebecca. Actually there
were twins, but before they were born, and long before they had
done anything morally significant, whether good or evil, God
shewed that His purpose must be worked out by His own selection and not as a reward of merit. For He said to Rebecca: 'The
elder shall serve the younger.' And the same position is stated
even more clearly in the text, 'I loved Jacob but hated Esau.'

[14] Well, does that mean that God is unjust? By no means.
You remember how He said to Moses, 'My own choice alone
shall dictate to whom I will show mercy and pity.' Everything
depends then not on our will, or our zeal, but on God's mercy.
For a further witness you may recall the words addressed to
Pharaoh: 'For this reason have I summoned you, that through
you I may make my power obvious, and that my character may
be understood throughout the world.' So then He has compassion on anyone He wishes, and anyone He wishes He makes
obdurate.

[19] You may say, 'Well, in that case what ground of complaint
has He against anyone, if no one can resist His will?' Dear man,
who are you to answer God? Can a piece of pottery say to the
potter, 'Why did you make me so?' Hasn't the potter authority
over the clay, so that out of the same batch he can make one
vessel for ornament and another for kitchen use? And how can
we grumble if God, wishing to reveal His power and make known
His anger, patiently put up with the vessels destined for wrath,
keeping them against the moment of their destruction, and at the
same time, wishing to display the wealth of His glory in the case
of the vessels destined for salvation, preserved them for the glory
that He had foreordained? To the latter class you and I belong,
whether we are Jews or non-Jews, because we have been chosen
by God. That is what the verse from Hosea means:

> I will call those my people who were not my people,
> And her beloved who had no lover.
> In the place where it was said,
> 'You are no people of mine,'
> There shall they be called
> 'Sons of the Living God.'

And as for the true Israel, Isaiah asserts. 'Though the number of Israelites were as the sand of the sea, only a remnant shall be saved; for God will execute a precise and summary sentence upon the earth.' And again, 'If Jehovah had not left us a few descendants we should have been wiped out like Sodom and Gomorrha.'

[30] What then is the conclusion? Why, that the non-Jews who never sought righteousness have found it, though a righteousness not of deeds but of faith, while the Israelites who followed the law of righteousness could never catch up with it. And why couldn't they? Precisely because they tried to do so on the ground of works rather than of faith. On that stumbling-block they tripped, and so fulfilled the well-known verse:

> On Zion I a stumbling-block install,
> 'Tis faith alone that shall escape a fall.

X

Why the Jews were Rejected

The Jews' salvation, brothers, is the dearest longing of my heart. I gladly acknowledge that they have a certain zeal for religion, but it is ill-informed. For they persist in ignoring the holiness offered by God and seeking to establish a holiness of their own. But Christ is the goal of the Law's struggle for holiness, and that is won only by believing. In the Pentateuch it says, 'He who seeks holiness on the basis of the Law must give his whole life to it.' But to one who aims at holiness by faith we should say: 'Do not ask in despair, Who can climb up into Heaven to bring Christ down, or who can climb down into Hades to bring Christ up from the dead? His word is near you already, in your heart and in your mouth. And that is the word of faith, which we proclaim.'

[9] You will be saved without doubt, if you are not afraid openly to confess that Jesus is Lord, and if you really believe in your heart that God did raise Him from the dead. For with the heart one believes and finds holiness, while with the lips one confesses and finds salvation. That is guaranteed by the Scripture which says, 'No one who believes in Him can ever be let down.'

[12] As for the relative position of Jew and Greek, no difference is made between them. The same Lord rules over both alike and is bountiful to all who seek His aid. '*Whosoever* invokes the help of the Lord will be saved.'

[14] But, you may ask, how can they invoke the aid of One in whom they do not believe? And how can they believe in One of whom they have never heard? And how can they hear if there is no one to preach? And how can anyone preach until he is sent? 'Happy indeed is the arrival of the messenger who brings Good News.'

[16] It is true that not everyone will accept the Good News. Even Isaiah asks, 'Lord, who has believed our message?' But there can be no faith if there is no opportunity of hearing the message, and there can be no opportunity of hearing unless there is someone to deliver the message. But was there no such opportunity? Certainly.

> Through the whole earth has sped their voice
> The farthest limits of the world rejoice.

Well, was it only Israel who failed to recognize the truth? That at least is what Moses suggests:

> To those who are no people of mine
>   By showing my favour,
> I will move you to jealous wrath
>   And be their Saviour.
> By means of a backward race
>   I will move you to rancour.

Isaiah speaks with even greater boldness.

> By those who sought me not
>> Have I been found:
> 'Mong those who asked not for me
>> Have I been renowned.

But in respect of Israel he says, 'All day long have I made overtures to an unresponsive and contradictory people.'

XI

The Rejection of the Jews is only Partial and Temporary

You must not take this as implying that God has finally abandoned His people. I am myself an Israelite, a lineal descendant of Abraham, a member of the clan of Benjamin. It is incredible that God should reject the people whom He foreordained. Remember the passage about Elijah, where he pleads with God against Israel: 'I am left all alone, and now they are trying to kill me.' And how does Jehovah answer? 'I have left for myself seven thousand men who have never bowed the knee to Baal.' Just so at the present moment there is left a faithful 'remnant', chosen beforehand by God's good grace.

[6] But if their position is the result of grace it is not a reward for any work that they have done. Otherwise a gift would be no longer a gift.

[7] Well then, what Israel sought she did not find: only the elect found it. The rest were hardened, as it says in the Bible, 'God has given them a spirit of frustration, eyes that are blind, and ears that fail to hear, up to this very moment.' And the Psalmist says:

> Let their table become a trap, a snare,
>> A stumbling-block, affliction rare.
> Blind Thou their eyes lest they shall see,
>> Bend their stiff neck 'neath Thy yoke-tree.

Does this then mean that they stumbled so badly as to fall altogether? By no means. Through their lapse, salvation has come to the Pagans in order that they themselves may be moved to emulation. But if their lapse spells wealth for the world and their loss means gain for the Pagans, whatever may we not expect from their enrichment?

[13] May I say one word to those readers who are not Jews. As an official messenger to the Pagans I make the most of my position. By so doing I hope that I shall provoke my own country-men to jealousy, and so save perhaps a few of them. If their rejection has involved reconciliation for the World, what will their acceptance mean but a general resurrection? To use an analogy: the dedication of the first sheaves consecrates the whole harvest. Or to put it another way: if the root is holy so must also the branches be. It is true that certain of the original branches were cut off, and that you, a mere slip of an olive, were grafted on in their place, so that you have now become part and parcel of the rich oil-bearing tree. But please don't crow over those other branches. If you do feel inclined to boast, let me remind you that you did not bear the root, but the root bears you.

[19] You may reply 'At any rate the branches were broken off and I was grafted on.' True. Because of their faithlessness they were broken off and you hold their place by faith. Don't be con-ceited about that. If God did not spare the natural branches, He will certainly not spare you. Understand then both the kindness and sternness of God: sternness to those who fall, kindness to you —so long as you respond to His kindness. Otherwise you will be cut off; and they, if they do not continue in unbelief, will be grafted on again. God is quite able to do that. If you, who by nature are a slip from a wild olive, can be taken contrary to nature and grafted on to a good olive, how much more easily can those who belong to it by nature be grafted on to a good olive?

[25] I wish you would try, my brothers, to penetrate this mystery. The attempt would forestall any tendency to self-conceit. The fact is this: Jewry has suffered a partial and temporary hardening of the heart, but only in order to allow time for the non-Jews to make up their number and achieve their

goal. When that has happened the way will be open to the salvation of all the Jews.

> From Zion the Saviour shall come
> The godless from Jewry to chase.
> With them I will banish your sins,
> A compact of love we will make.

So it was really for your sakes that the Jews were allowed to be hostile to the Gospel. But God's plan to work by selection still stands, and as far as that is concerned the Jews are still reckoned among the specially privileged for the Patriarchs' sakes. There is nothing capricious about God's calling or His favours.

[30] As you were once disobedient to God, but have now been shewn mercy through their disobedience, so they are now disobedient in anticipation of a similar act of mercy. God, you see, has allowed all to be guilty of disobedience in order that He may have mercy upon all. O what wealth of wisdom and knowledge is in God! How inscrutable are His judgments and unsearchable His ways!

> The mind of God who yet hath known
> Or tried to change His will?
> Who dared to furnish Him supplies
> And offer Him a bill?

Everything is His already. The whole universe comes from Him; through Him it is sustained in being; to Him it returns as its final goal. Glory to Him for ever. Amen.

XII

You must not be superior, but behave with Christian Love

I pray you, therefore, brethren, because of these Divine mercies, to offer yourselves as a living and holy sacrifice, very pleasing to God. That is the most intelligent service you can render Him. Don't allow yourselves to be spoilt by your environment, but rather let your character be transformed by the remoulding of your whole attitude of mind. Only so will you be

able to judge accurately what is God's will and what in His eyes
is good, pleasing and perfect.

[3] I am bound to warn you officially against the danger of
assuming superiority. Don't presume upon your privileges, or
look down upon others. Cultivate sober thoughts, according to
the degree of faith that God has granted to each one. Every
person has his own proper place and function. Take the example
of our physical organism; there is only one body, but it has a
variety of limbs each with its own particular function. So in the
Church we are all members of one another and form only one
body in Christ, but we have each our own peculiar part to play.
For God gives different gifts to each one. Let us each use our
gifts to the full. If we have been given the ability to prophesy,
let us prophesy to the full limit of our faith. If welfare-work is
our special sphere let us busy ourselves in the service of others.
If we are teachers, let us concentrate on teaching. If we are
orators, let us inspire comfort and good counsel.

[8] In the same way, if you are bestowing charity, do it from a
wholly disinterested motive. If you are in a position of authority,
don't be slack, but shew yourself alert. If you are visiting the
sick and the poor, carry about with you an atmosphere of cheer-
fulness. Be truly loving without simulating an affection you do
not feel. Set yourselves deliberately to hate evil and to admire
the good. Let real affection vitalize your devotion to the common
interests of the brethren. Try to obtain recognition for others
rather than for yourselves. The Lord's journeyman must be
business-like, full of enthusiasm, optimistic, patient in adversity,
keen about his prayers, willing to share his goods with needy
brethren, ready to show hospitality to strangers. Speak good of
those who torment you, good and not evil. Cultivate a ready
sympathy both with the happy and with the miserable. Try to
share in the common thoughts and aspirations of the rest. Don't
be social climbers but associate with the humble. Don't be
superior. Never pay back evil for evil, but let people see you are
always working for the highest ends. As far as you can, live at
peace with all. Don't be anxious, my friends, to 'get your own
back', but be willing to ignore the other fellow's anger. You
know what Jehovah said, 'It is my business to exact vengeance;

I will do the paying back.' If your enemy is hungry feed him; if he is thirsty give him something to drink. The knowledge that you so befriended him will prick his conscience like a burning flame. We must not let evil overwhelm us but we must overwhelm evil with good.

XIII

The Present Crisis demands specially careful Conduct

All of us should be duly subordinate to authority. For authority derives ultimately from God, and therefore those who exercise it are in a real sense appointed by Him. It follows that the man who resists authority is in rebellion against the ordinance of God. And he who rebels must expect punishment.

[3] It is not honesty, but only crime, that needs to fear the police. Do you wish to walk undismayed in the sight of authority? Then be honourable in all your dealings and you will receive nothing but praise. The magistrate is God's agent for your benefit. But if you do wrong you may well be afraid, for you will find that 'the sword of justice' is no mere figure of speech, but the magistrate will turn out to be God's agent to inflict vengeance on the wrong-doer.

[5] So then it is doubly necessary that we carefully watch our behaviour, first from fear of a possible penalty, and then for the sake of our own conscience. Actually the reason why we pay taxes is that Government attends to this very matter on our behalf. In so doing it discharges a duty imposed by God. As far as our individual conduct is concerned we should be considerate to all with whom we have any dealings. We should be prompt to pay our rates and taxes when they fall due; and we should be ready to pay respect and reverence where *they* are due.

[8] Owe no debt to anyone except that of love. The man who loves keeps the whole Law. Those well-known commandments: 'Thou shalt not commit adultery; thou shalt do no murder; thou shalt not steal; thou shalt not covet'; and all the rest of them, are completely summed up in the one saying, 'Thou shalt love

thy neighbour as thyself.' Love cannot do any harm to its neighbours, therefore love is the fulfilment of the whole Law.

[11] The critical nature of our age gives a special importance to all this. The moment of our final deliverance is a good deal nearer than when we were first converted. The night is all but over; the dawn is breaking. It is time to wake up! We must shed all dark deeds and clothe ourselves with the shining armour of day. In the full light of this new age, let us give special care to our conduct. There must be no drinking parties, no outrageous flirtations (let alone anything worse), no quarrels, no jealous tiffs. Clothe yourselves with the character of the Lord Jesus Christ, and don't worry about your physical nature to fulfil its too ardent desires.

XIV

We must respect one another's Scruples

If a scrupulous person wishes to join you, welcome him into your circle but don't treat him to a lot of logic-chopping discussions. You may have trouble with such at table. A person of robust faith will eat whatever is put before him, but a scrupulous man may think that he must be a vegetarian. Well, the former should not despise the latter, nor the latter be criticized by the former. After all, God has received the weak-minded person, and there is room for both in the Church. It is a point of good manners not to criticize someone else's servant; he holds his position solely by grace of his own master. And even the scrupulous will manage to retain their position, for their Master can give them strength to do so.

[5] Another difficulty may arise out of the observance of fasts and festivals. One man distinguishes between the sacredness of different days, while another regards every day as equally holy. Well, let each man think the thing out for himself and stand by his own conclusion. If a man observes a particular day, he keeps it not for the benefit of other people but to the honour of God. In the same way, whatever we eat we do it to the glory of God, for it is to Him that we say our grace. None of us can say that

what he does is entirely his own concern. None of us lives or dies merely for himself. If we live, we live to the Lord; if we die it is at the Lord's command. Therefore whether we live or die we are the Lord's. That is the reason why Christ died and came to life again, that He might be Lord both of the dead and of the living.

[10]   Why then should you criticize your brother, or why should you look down on him? God alone will ultimately judge us all. 'As I live,' saith the Lord, 'every knee shall bend to me; and every tongue shall make public confession of faith in God.' Obviously then each one of us must answer for himself before God.

[13]   Let's not criticize one another. But let us be meticulously careful not to put an obstacle or a stumbling-block in our brother's way. I hold it for certain on the ground of our Christian faith that absolutely nothing is by its own nature taboo. But if a man thinks that something is 'unclean', for him it is unclean. Consequently if you let your brother's conscience be wounded by some food that you eat, you are not behaving charitably. Don't allow your food to destroy a man for whom Christ died. The privilege you enjoy is not worth a scandal. After all, the Kingdom of God is not made up of eating and drinking; it consists of righteousness and peace and joy in the Holy Ghost. Only he who serves Christ in this way is pleasing to God and respected by men.

[19]   Let us then cultivate such conduct as leads to peace and mutual edification. Do not for the sake of food let down the work of God. Everything is 'clean', but it becomes unclean for a man who is scandalized by what he eats. It is better not to eat flesh or to drink wine, or to do anything that proves a stumbling-block to your brother. Preserve your own conviction between yourself and God. You will be happy in not having anything of which to accuse your own conscience. But he who has misgivings is condemned if he eats, because he does not do it out of conviction. Whatever we do without honest conviction is always sin.

XV

Let all sections live together in Mutual Helpfulness

We that are strong ought to support the weak and infirm, and not do just what we please. Let us each try to please our neighbour so that we can do him good and build up his character. Christ did not please Himself. As the Book says, 'The insults that were heaped on Thee have fallen upon Me.'

[4] Such prophetic passages were written to instruct us, so that through perseverance and through the comfort drawn from the Scriptures we may acquire confidence. May the God who inspires such perseverance and comfort bring you into agreement with one another in accordance with the mind of Christ Jesus, so that in unison of heart and voice you may sing the glories of the God and Father of our Lord Jesus Christ.

[7] To this end give a cordial welcome to one another as Christ welcomed us, to the glory of God. I venture to say that that is the very reason why Christ served His ministry under the Law of circumcision, to vindicate the truthfulness of God by fulfilling the promises made to the Patriarchs and at the same time make the Pagans glorify God for His mercy. Several passages of Scripture enforce the lesson: 'For this reason will I acknowledge Thee among the Pagans and sing praise to Thy Name.' Again, 'Rejoice, ye Pagans, in company with His own people.' And once more:

> Praise the Lord, O ye Pagans
> And praise Him all ye nations.

And Isaiah says:

> 'Jesse's Scion shall be there,
> Within whose rule the Pagans come.
> Their hope on Him is fixed.'

The God of hope fill you with all joy and peace in this belief, that you may be confident in hope through the power of the Holy Spirit.

Impending Visit

[14] As far as I am concerned I have no doubts on your account. You are thoroughly kind-hearted, very knowledgeable, and well able to advise one another. However, I have taken my courage in both hands to remind you of the divine commission given me to act as Christ's minister to the non-Jews. It is my business to perform the rites of the Gospel for them, so that they may be presented to God, as an acceptable offering, consecrated by the Holy Spirit.

[17] I can express real pride in the success through Christ Jesus of my evangelistic work. I will not venture to speak of anything except what Christ has actually done through my own instrumentality by way of bringing the Pagans to His allegiance. Marvellous signs have been granted to reinforce my words and deeds, and that could only have been by the power of the Holy Spirit. By this means all the way from Jerusalem and its environs right up to Illyricum I have proclaimed the gospel of Christ in all its fullness.

[20] Personally I have made it my ambition to preach the gospel only where it had not been heard before. I did not want to build on another man's foundation. I preferred to act in the spirit of the words:

> They shall see Him who no vision yet have seen,
> And they who have not heard shall understand.

That is why I have so long abstained from coming to see you. But now there is no further opening for me in these parts; and for some years I have had a keen desire to visit you if ever I went to Spain. I hope that now I am to pass through I shall see you, and that you will set me on my way after I have enjoyed your hospitality for a little while.

[25] At the moment however I am on my way to Jerusalem to perform an errand of mercy for our members there. Macedonia and Achaia have been good enough to make a collection on behalf of the poor among the Christians in Jerusalem. They were glad to do it because they know themselves to be actually the

brethren's debtors. And indeed it is right that if the Pagans have shared in the brethren's spiritual advantages, they should minister to the brethren's needs in material things.

[28] When I have completed the business and handed over these alms to the beneficiaries, I shall come to you on my way to Spain. I feel sure that when I do I shall bring with me the full blessing of Christ. And I do hope, my brethren, that you will pray very earnestly for me; indeed I solemnly urge you to do so for the sake of our Lord Jesus Christ and by the love of the Holy Spirit, in order that I may be delivered from the unbelievers in Judea and that my mission in Jerusalem may prove acceptable to the brethren. If that turns out so, I shall come to you in a very happy frame of mind; and with you, if God wills, I shall find rest awhile. The God of peace be with you all. Amen.

XVI

Final Greeting and Warning

I commend to your hospitality Phœbe, one of our sisters and a deaconess of the Church in Cenchrea. Give her a proper Christian welcome and assist her in every way necessary. She has been a comfort to many, including myself.

[3] Give my greetings to Priscilla and Aquila, my colleagues in the work of Christ, who have actually risked their lives to save mine. For their devotion all the non-Jewish Churches join with me in offering sincerest thanks. I send greetings also to the congregation that meets in their house.

[5] Remember me to my dear friend Epaenetus, who was the first person to be converted in the Province of Asia, and also to Mary who has worked so hard for you. My kindest regards to Andronicus and Junia, who are not only fellow-countrymen of mine but were also my fellow-prisoners; they have earned a great reputation among the Apostles; and indeed they were converted to Christianity before I was. Remember me to Amplias, for whom I have a very deep and very Christian regard; to Urban my fellow-worker in Christ; to Stachys my dear friend; and to Apelles, who is so uncompromising a Christian.

[10]   Give my greetings also to Aristobulus and his family, to Herodion my fellow-countryman, to the Christian members of Narcissus' household, to Tryphaena and Tryphosa who work so hard for the Church, and to my friend Persis, who also is a hard-worker.

[13]   My kind regards to that outstanding Christian Rufus, and to his mother who also mothered me. Best wishes also to Asyncritus, Phlegon, Hermes, Patrobas, Hermas and all the brothers with them. Don't forget Philologus, Julia, Nereus and his sister, and Olympas and all the brethren with them. Embrace one another for me at the Kiss of Peace. All the Christian churches send you greetings.

[17]   But I must solemnly warn you, brothers, to look out for those who cause divisions and scandals contrary to the teaching that you have learnt. Have no dealings with them; for they do not serve our Lord Christ but their own selfish ends. With specious and plausible words they turn the hearts of the innocent. But your loyalty has come to everyone's ears. I am very happy on your account, but I should like you to be well versed in everything that is good and unversed in all that is evil. The God of peace will soon crush Satan under your feet.

The Grace of our Lord Jesus be with you.

[21]   My colleague Timothy wishes to add his greetings. So also do my relatives Lucius, Jason and Sosipater. Tertius, the amanuensis who is actually taking down this letter adds his greetings in his own hand. Gaius, who is host not only to me but to the whole Church, sends his respects; as also do Brother Quartus and Erastus the City Treasurer.

[25]   To God all-wise be glory
             Who strength hath given to men
        By making known His secret
             Long hid from human ken.

        Prophetic voices told it
             To ears that closed again,
        But now to faithful Pagans
             He makes the mystery plain.

8

Colossians

The town of Colosse was destroyed by earthquake a few years after this letter was written. It was situated on the Lycus in Phrygia, and was thus near the scene of Paul's missionary labours. He was not himself responsible for the foundation of the church there: that honour belonged to his disciple Epaphras, who, with others of their circle, appears to have done much work in outlying districts while the leader was busy in Ephesus.

Although he never visited the place, Paul felt himself responsible for the welfare of its church, and while he was a prisoner in Rome he wrote this letter as the result of news brought to him by Epaphras. There was much in the progress made by the Colossian Christians for which to be thankful, but they were in danger from a new kind of false teaching. Oriental fondness for esoteric systems had led some of them to develop a kind of 'superior' Christianity. They encouraged circumcision, not as necessary to salvation, but as conducive to perfection. They also practised a cult of angels (Thrones, Lordships, Rulers and Powers), and emphasized the importance of advanced knowledge (wisdom, or 'Gnosis'). These facts have led scholars to conclude that the false teachers were precursors of the notorious Gnostics who later gave much trouble to the authorities of the Church.

S. Paul does not discourage the desire for true Gnosis, but insists that such knowledge has been given once for all by Christ, Who is the sole agent of creation and the only Head of the Church. There is, therefore, no need for Christians to occupy themselves with lesser supernatural beings.

In the latter part of the epistle Paul, following the example of many religious and philosophical teachers of the day, outlines a code of morals, giving rules for the conduct of Christians in various states of life.

A Letter To The Faithful Members
Of The Church At Colosse

I

My dear Brethren,

This letter comes to you from Paul, whom you know to be an Apostle of Jesus Christ, duly accredited by the will of God, and also from Brother Timothy. We wish you grace and peace from God our Father.

Gratitude for Progress

[3] We are always thanking God, the Father of our Lord Jesus Christ, when we mention you in our prayers, because we have heard so much of your loyalty to Christ Jesus and of the love you have shown to all the brethren. I am sure you still keep in mind the hope stored up for you as a treasure in Heaven, about which you were told when you first heard the true Gospel preached. That Gospel is bearing fruit and expanding throughout all the civilized world, as it does among yourselves and has done from the day when you first heard it and recognized the truth about the grace of God. It was in its proper form that you received the Gospel, not from false teachers, but from our dear colleague, Epaphras, who is Christ's faithful minister to you. He has now brought me definite news of the love you display in the Spirit.

Prayer for future advance

[9] Since hearing this news we have never ceased offering prayers and supplications that you may be filled with a thorough knowledge of God's will in all wisdom and spiritual understanding, that your conduct may be so worthy of the Lord as thoroughly to please Him, and that you may show the fruit of a Christian life in every kind of good deed while still advancing in the knowledge of God. We pray too that you may be reinforced with all

the strength there is by means of His glorious power, so that you may be able to suffer and endure everything not merely without complaint but with actual joy, giving thanks the while to the Father who has made it possible for you to claim your share of the inheritance with the Saints in the Kingdom of Light. It was He who rescued us out of the power of darkness and established us as citizens in the Kingdom of His beloved Son, through whom we enjoy redemption and remission of sins.

The Person of Christ and His Work

[15] Jesus is the visible representative of the invisible God, the Father's first born and Prince of the whole creation. Through Him the universe was created, everything in heaven and on earth, visible and invisible, and all supernatural beings such as Thrones, Lordships, Rulers and Powers. Everything was created through Him and for Him. He existed before everything and everything derives its being from Him.

[18] He is also the Head of the divine Body, the Church. In Him we Christians have made a new beginning, for He is the first-born from the dead, which makes Him our Superior in every respect. And this supremacy is His because God willed that in Him the plenitude of Deity should have its abode, and that through Him He should reconcile the universe to Himself. This God has done by making the blood of His cross the means of establishing peace, so effecting through Him a restoration of all things both in earth and heaven.

[21] You yourselves were once estranged from God, and were wickedly hostile to Him both in thought and deed. But now in Christ's body you have been reconciled to God through His physical death, and you have been presented to God holy and unblemished and free from any charge—so long of course as you remain firmly rooted in the faith as you originally received it, and have not deviated from that hopeful Gospel of which I Paul am a minister and which has now been preached throughout the whole creation under heaven.

[24] I am glad of my suffering on your behalf. By it I am helping in my own person to make up the full complement of

Christ's suffering on behalf of His body the Church. I became a minister of the Church through the commission given me by God for your benefit. It is my duty to preach fully the word of God, and to explain the mystery of His design, which has been concealed from past ages and generations, but has now been revealed to the members of His Church. God determined to make known to them in all its glorious richness the secret of His purpose in respect of all persons of non-Jewish race. And that secret is that Christ the Messiah is for you too the hope of glory. It is such a Messiah that we proclaim. We warn and instruct every human being without distinction or reserve in accordance with the full divine teaching, in order that we may present every man perfectly trained in Christ. To this end I toil and struggle with all the energy which He has so powerfully infused into me.

II

I should like you to know the magnitude of the struggle in which I am engaged on your behalf and on behalf of the Laodiceans, and indeed of all who have never met me face to face. I am striving that they may be encouraged to persevere, that they may be united in love, that they may be brought to the full and firm conviction which springs from a rich understanding and may be led to a complete comprehension of God's secret, which is nothing less than Christ, in whom all the treasures of wisdom and knowledge lie concealed.

Warning against Error.

[4] I am telling you this in order that no one may delude you by specious arguments. Even though I am absent in the flesh, I am certainly with you in the spirit; and I am very happy at the thought of the good order and the solidarity you maintain by your faith in Christ.

[6] Continue to order your conduct under the lordship of Christ Jesus as you accepted it from Epaphras. I should like to see you firmly rooted in Christ, built up from hour to hour in Him, growing ever stronger in the faith as you have been taught it,

your hearts overflowing all the time with thankfulness. See that you do not fall a prey to any hollow and misleading philosophizing, spun out of mere human and childish traditions about supernatural beings and quite alien from the teaching of Christ. In Him alone abides all the perfection of the Godhead in bodily form. And you are perfected in Him, for He is the Head over every supernatural Rule and Authority. In Him and in His circumcision you have received a spiritual circumcision even while rejecting the literal circumcision of the flesh, for in baptism you have been dead and buried with Him and have risen again with Him through faith in that Divine power which raised Him from the dead. You who were dead in sin and had no literal circumcision to rely on were 'quickened' by Christ so as to live together with Him. He forgave us all our sins and expunged from the Law all the rigmarole of regulations that had been entered up against us. This He swept out of sight and nailed to His cross. And at the same time he stripped away like a cast-off garment every demonic Rule and Authority and made a public exhibition of them, openly triumphing over them on the cross.

[16] Therefore let no one criticize you in respect of meat or drink, or the keeping of a feast, or the observance of a new moon or a Sabbath Day. Such regulations were only shadows thrown in advance by events to come. The solid reality has arrived in Christ. Don't let anyone jockey you out of your prize with a lot of finicking regulations about acts of humility and prostration to angels, taking his stand upon alleged visions, inflated with vain and sensuous fancies, instead of holding fast to the one Head, which is Christ. It is only by maintaining our connection with Him that the whole Body, regularly served and compacted into a unity by its joints and sinews, can steadily increase and add to its divine growth.

[20] Through your unity with Christ you have already died to the elemental crudities of this world. Why then do you lay down pettifogging rules for yourselves as if you were still living for this world, such as 'Touch not! Taste not! Handle not!' All such prohibitions deal with material things, which fade out of existence as soon as they are used. The precepts they embody are just man-made teachings—no more. They acquire a reputation for

belonging to a higher order of thought because they include self-imposed practices, acts of humility, and asceticism, but they are of no real value to check sensual indulgence.

III

The New Life in Christ

Since then you have risen with Christ, aim at the things that really do belong to the higher life, that life in which Christ is already enthroned, seated at the right hand of God. Give your thoughts to the things that belong to that sphere, and not to the mere material world. After all you have died, and your life is hid with Christ in God. When Christ, who is our life, appears again, then we shall be seen to accompany Him in glory.

[5] So you must really put to death that part of you which belongs exclusively to this world—fleshly sin, impurity, passion, evil lust, and the unrestrained desire that amounts to idolatry. It is such things that arouse the wrath of God. And you did practise such things once, when you lived in the midst of them. But now you must put away in addition all sorts of other sins—passionate anger, maliciousness, swearing, loose talk. Cleanse your life of such things. Don't deceive one another, but put off the old nature with its characteristic practices and put on the new, in which the image of its Creator is always being renewed and perfected as our knowledge of Him increases. In that likeness there is no room for distinction between Greek and Jew, circumcised and uncircumcised, between barbarian, Scythian, slave and free, but Christ is all in all.

[12] As is natural then to men who are chosen out by God, dedicated to Him and beloved by Him, clothe yourselves with pity, kindness, humility, gentleness, patience. If anyone has a complaint against another, let him be forbearing and forgiving. As the Lord has forgiven you, you must forgive one another. And to this add the supreme grace of love, which binds us all together in the perfect life. Let the need to maintain a truly Christian peace be the arbiter in all your emotions, for to that have we all been summoned in one body—a fact for which we must be supremely thankful.

[16] Let the word of Christ have a treasured place in your hearts. Teach and instruct one another in every kind of wisdom. Sing psalms and hymns and songs of the spiritual life with heartfelt thankfulness to God. Whatever you do in word or deed, do it all in the name of the Lord Jesus, giving thanks to God the Father through Him.

Moral Code

[18] Wives, be submissive to your husbands, as is fitting for Christians.

Husbands, love your wives and don't get exasperated with them.

Children, obey your parents in everything, for that is what is expected of a Christian.

Fathers, don't provoke your children, else they will lose heart.

Slaves, obey your earthly masters in everything, not merely when they are looking at you, as if you wanted to please men only, but whole-heartedly out of respect for the heavenly Master. Whatever you do, put your whole soul into it, as if you were doing it for the Lord and not for men. You know that from Him at least you will receive full and proper payment, nothing less than the legacy He has won for us. The Lord Christ is your Master. Therefore he who does wrong, slave or owner, will pay the penalty. There is no favouritism with God.

IV

Masters, treat your slaves in a just and equitable fashion. Remember that you yourselves have a Master in Heaven.

[2] Persevere with your prayers, and keep your attention from wandering by mingling them with thanksgiving. And in the midst of all your other petitions, don't forget a prayer also for us—that God may open up opportunities for preaching about that secret of the Christian revelation, for proclaiming which I have been thrown into prison. Pray that it may be made clear to me how I ought to speak. Be circumspect in your approach to any who do not belong to us, but make the most of every opportunity. Let your conversation always have in it a seasoning of

Christian grace, and study what kind of an answer to give to each individual.

[7]   All my personal news will be brought to you by Tychicus, my dear brother and faithful attendant and fellow-servant in the Lord. I am sending him to you for this very purpose, so that when you know how we have fared, you may be comforted and relieved. With him I am sending Onesimus, another loyal and beloved brother, who actually belongs to your part of the world. They will tell you all that has taken place here.

[10]   Greetings from Aristarchus, my comrade in arms, and Mark, a cousin of Barnabas. (One special instruction about him; if he visits you, make him welcome). Greetings also from Jesus who is called Justus. These three are the only members of the circumcision party who are working with us for the spread of the Kingdom, and they have been a great comfort to me. Your old friend, Epaphras, a true slave of Jesus Christ, wishes to be remembered to you. In our Intercession services, he is always most exercised on your behalf, praying that you may hold your ground like mature and fully convinced Christians, in obedience to the will of God. I can assure you that he shows great zeal on your behalf and on behalf of our brothers in Laodicea and Hierapolis.

[14]   Dear Dr. Luke sends greetings and so does Demas. Convey our best wishes to the brethren in Laodicea and to Nymphas and to the congregation which meets in his house.

[16]   When this letter has been read to you, see that it is also read in the Church of the Laodiceans, while you read the one that I have sent to Laodicea. Here is a special message for Archippus. 'See that you do not fail to exercise the Ministry that has been committed to you by the Lord.'

[18]   My own greetings I add in my own writing, and with my own signature. Don't forget me in my prison.

Grace be with you,

Paul

Ephesians

The letter to the Colossians was not the only epistle carried by Tychicus and Onesimus from Paul, prisoner in Rome, to a church in Asia Minor. There was also one to Laodicea, a town about twelve miles to the west of Colosse. Some scholars, both ancient and modern, have judged it to be identical with our 'Ephesians'. Certainly the name Ephesus is omitted from the address of this epistle in certain important manuscripts. A favourite view at the present time is that 'Ephesians' is a circular letter meant to be read in a number of churches, including those of Laodicea and Hierapolis, and that the address was purposely left blank so that the appropriate name might be inserted by the reader for each congregation.

The very nature of such an 'encyclical' removes it from the sphere of purely local controversy and makes a more general treatment of common topics both possible and necessary. While the same ideas as had been dealt with in Colossians were still running in S. Paul's mind when he wrote this letter, he is here able to give a more positive and serene expression to his teaching. Especially with regard to the 'mystery' of God's purpose in history and the new life in the Church he reaches a joyous sublimity which is scarcely to be found elsewhere even in the New Testament. The renewed emphasis on a Moral Code for Christians should also be noticed.

S. Paul's Letter To The Ephesians

Paul to the Church in [Ephesus]

I

My dear, faithful fellow-Christians,

I must begin by reminding you of my credentials. I am one who has been appointed, through a special revelation of the will of God, as an Apostle of Christ Jesus. This letter conveys my cordial greetings and assurance of my prayers that you may be granted the gifts of grace and peace from God our Father and the Lord Jesus Christ.

God's Secret Purpose now revealed to Jew and Gentile alike

[3] Blessed be the God and Father of our Lord Jesus Christ who has Himself blessed us through Christ with every kind of spiritual and supernatural blessing. He actually pre-selected us in Christ before the foundation of the world in order that we should be holy and without blemish in His eyes. In His love he foreordained us through Jesus Christ to adoption into His family. And that He did simply at His own good pleasure and of His own will; a fact that surely redounds to the credit of His splendid graciousness.

[7] His grace He has bestowed upon us in Jesus the Beloved, who has procured Redemption for us, that is the remission of our sins, at the price of His own life. How rich is the kindness that He has showered upon us in disclosing to us a complete explanation of His secret purpose. (That again was entirely due to His own good pleasure, which He manifested beforehand in Christ). His purpose was to make all history work out towards one culminating moment, when He could bring every movement in the whole universe, spiritual as well as material, to a head in Christ.

[11] We Jewish Christians have a share in the working out of this purpose, for having been set apart beforehand for this honour

in accordance with the design of God, who works out everything by His own deliberate purpose, we have now been called by Christ. So we Christians of Jewish birth shall bring credit to His glory because we have been the first to set our hope on Christ.

[13] And now you too, who are not of Jewish birth, have listened to the word of truth, the Good News of His salvation. You too have believed in Him and have been confirmed by the long-promised gift of His Holy Spirit. And that fact is in itself a guarantee that one day all, whom God has marked out for His own, shall be redeemed, and so bring additional credit to His glory.

A Prayer for Fuller Knowledge

[15] From the moment I heard of your faith in the Lord Jesus and of your love towards all the Brethren I have never ceased thanking God for you. I have also mentioned you in my intercessions, asking that the God of our Lord Jesus Christ, the Father of Glory, will give you the Spirit of Wisdom, who is also the Spirit of Revelation, that you may learn to know Him thoroughly. May He enlighten the eyes of your hearts so that you may know how great is the hope His calling brings, how rich His glorious inheritance among the Brethren, and how tremendous the possibilities of His power in us who believe. The measure of His might and strength was displayed in the case of Jesus whom He raised from the dead. Him He made to sit on His right hand in Heaven far above all potentates, authorities, powers, lordships, and every other title that can be given either in this world or in that to come.

[22] 'He hath put the universe under His feet.' In so exalting Christ He has made Him Head of a Body, the Church. That Body provides a universal means of expression for one who is Himself a universal Personality.

II

Sin and Salvation

There was a time when you too were dead like Jesus, only not in a tomb, but in trespasses and sins. For that is how you used to conduct yourselves in accordance with the habits of this present world under allegiance to the Prince of the Power of the Air, the spirit that still rules among those who do not acknowledge the reign of God.

[3]   In similar depravity we Jews also lived at one time, given up to carnal desires, pursuing sensual aims and purposes: and we were the fit object of divine wrath like the rest. But God, who is rich in mercy, for the great love He bore us even while we were dead in sin, raised us together with Christ to a new life and made us live with Him and established us with Him in the heavenly sphere. So you see that it is of God's free gift that we have been saved. And through the ages still to come He will give further proof of the amazing riches of His grace in the kindness He will yet show to us in Christ Jesus.

[8]   I repeat that it is of God's free gift that you are saved in response to faith. It is not the result of anything you do, but the gift of God. It is not given in payment for any work of ours; and so none of us has any right to take credit to himself. We are what God has made us; and we have been created in Christ Jesus with a view to the good works that God has prepared beforehand for us to practise.

[11]   Don't forget then that as far as race is concerned you are Gentiles, to whom was attached the opprobrious epithet of 'Uncircumcised' by those who describe themselves as 'the Circumcision'—because forsooth they have submitted to a surgical operation. And don't forget that at that time you were living apart from Christ and were also outlaws from the commonwealth of Israel and foreigners to the promise under the Covenant. You were without God and without a hope in the world.

[13]   But now in Christ Jesus you who once were such outsiders have been brought into the very heart of things by His self-sacrifice. He Himself is our peace. He has broken down the dividing wall that separated Jew from Gentile. He has abrogated the Law with all its detailed regulations. And He has made the two races one. Out of two distinct individuals He has, so to speak, by uniting both with Himself, created one new man. Thus

He has established peace and has put an end to the old hostility
by reconciling both to God through the offering of His own body
on the cross.

[17] In this way He came and proclaimed peace both to you
who were estranged and also to those who are more closely
related to Himself. Through Him we both alike have freedom of
access by the same Spirit to the Father. So you are no longer
foreigners, or even licensed immigrants, you now enjoy rights of
equal citizenship with the Brethren and with the members of
God's own household. You are part and parcel of the one building whose foundation consists of the Apostles and prophets and
whose key-stone is Jesus Himself. In Him each constituent part
of the building makes its own contribution to the completion of
a holy temple. In Him you yourselves form a section of God's
own spiritual habitation.

III

Paul's position as exponent of the Secret

Let me remind you again that I am in prison for my faith in
Christ and on behalf of you non-Jews. I suppose you have heard
that God has made me the steward of His grace in respect of you,
and that by special revelation He has made known to me His
hidden purpose. I have already said a word about that. As you
read it you can understand that I am versed in the mystery of
Christ. In earlier ages it was not made known to human beings,
but it has now been revealed to His holy Apostles and prophets
by the Spirit. The gist of the revelation is that the Pagans have
become fellow-heirs, fellow-members, and fellow-sharers in the
promise given by Christ Jesus through the Gospel. Of that
Gospel I was made a minister by the gift of God's grace conveyed
to me through the working of His power.

[8] To me, who am utterly inferior to all the Brethren, was this
gift granted, to proclaim to the Pagans the inexhaustible wealth
of Christ, and to make clear to them what has been kept secret
for long ages by the Divine Creator of the universe, namely, the
precise manner in which His plan is to be worked out. The

purpose of the concealment was that now at last through the instrumentality of the Church even the angelic Rulers and Powers in the heavenly sphere might learn fresh lessons in the intricate pattern of the Divine Wisdom revealed in the plan of the ages, which He had made in Christ Jesus our Lord. It is as we have faith in Him that we can play our own part in this plan with boldness and confidence. I trust therefore that you will not lose heart because of the troubles I suffer on your account. You might rather reflect that they do you honour.

[14] But to resume. The thought of all this brings me to my knees in prayer to God the Father. (It is from His Fatherhood that all paternal relationships, whether spiritual or physical, derive their name and character.) I pray then that out of the wealth of His glory He will grant you to be mightily strengthened by His Spirit in the very core of your being, and that in response to your faith Christ will take up his abode in your hearts. Then you will be deeply rooted and securely grounded in love, and you will be strong enough with the rest of the Brethren to grasp in all its breadth and length and height and depth the conception of the love of Christ. That is a subject of knowledge which surpasses knowledge. Nevertheless through it you will attain to the complete measure of the Wholeness which is God.

[20] Now to Him who is able to do not only what I have asked but things far beyond our asking or conceiving, by reason of His power that is at work in you, to Him be glory in the Church and in Christ Jesus for ever and ever world without end. Amen.

IV

New Life in the One Church

Now that you know God's plan let me earnestly entreat you, prisoner though I am, to make your conduct befit your Christian vocation. Be humble, gentle, patient. Support one another in love. Be careful to maintain your spiritual unity with one another by refusing to jeopardize your harmonious relations. Both sections of you, Jews and non-Jews, belong to one Body and one Spirit, just as one and the same hope was set before you both alike

when you were first converted. Similarly you have one only
Lord, one Faith, one Baptism, one God and Father of all who is
immanent in all and transcendent over all.
[7] To each of us has been given abundant grace up to the full
extent of Christ's generosity.

> The Victor mounting to His throne
> Is followed by a captive train
> And spoils of war distributes.

That phrase 'mounting to His throne', what does it imply but
that He first came down to this lower earth? The One who came
down is the same as the One who mounted up. He ascended to
the very highest heaven in order that He might fill the whole
universe. The 'spoils of war' that He distributed to mankind
are the varied gifts of the sacred ministry—Apostles, prophets,
evangelists, pastors and teachers. These gifts are intended to
equip the brethren for ministerial work so that the whole body
of the Church may be edified. In this way we shall all attain to
that unity which proceeds from the one faith and from the
knowledge of God's Son, and which is expressed in a perfect
manhood, the full stature of the wholeness of Christ.

[14] Thus we shall no longer be infants with unstable minds,
buffeted and wind-tossed by every changing fashion of doctrine,
at the mercy of men's deceitful juggling with words and their
singular dexterity in devising error. But by nourishing truth
with love we shall in every way grow up to the maturity of Christ
who is our Head. From Him the whole body, compact and knit
together through the contribution made by each part and through
the harmonious co-operation of each several member, grows as
an organic unity and builds up itself in love.

[17] This then is what I mean, and I must repeat it as solemnly
as I can, that you ought no longer to behave as the unconverted
Pagans do. Empty-minded, bemused in their intellect, estranged
from the vital power of God, through sheer ignorance and
obduracy they have callously surrendered themselves to licentiousness, displaying a perfect passion for the business of impurity.

[20] But that is not how you learnt your lesson from Christ. You have indeed listened to Him and have been taught by Him as He really is in Jesus, the very embodiment of truth. From Him you learnt that your duty is to drop your former manner of life, to strip off the old nature like a garment decayed by deceitful passions, and then to be renovated in your innermost self, and so to clothe yourselves with a new nature created after the Divine pattern in all the righteousness and holiness of truth.

[25] Begin then by abstaining from falsehood and by sticking to the truth in all intercourse with your neighbours. It would be absurd for one member of a body to try to deceive another. Don't let anger be carried to the point of sin by nursing it all day. It is when we are in a sulky frame of mind that the devil has his greatest opportunity. Let the pilferer give up his thieving and let him take to good honest labour. In that way he may have something to give to a needy neighbour. Let no salacious word pass your lips, but let your conversation be of an edifying character so that those who listen may get some good out of it. Be careful not to distress the Holy Spirit of God whom you received at your Confirmation, and by whom you will be kept until the Day of Redemption. Put an end to all bitterness, hard thoughts, anger, loud words, injurious talk, and every kind of maliciousness. Be kind to one another, compassionate, and generous, as God has been generous to you in Christ.

V

Further conduct proper to the New Life

What you have to do is to imitate God as children imitate their parents. Surround yourself with an atmosphere of love, for Christ loved you so much as to give Himself up to death on your behalf, truly a fragrant offering and sacrifice to God.

[3] Such subjects as immorality or any kind of impurity or lust should never be canvassed among you. The Christian's conversation is free from those matters. To him such things as obscenity, buffoonery, or mere facetiousness are all alike unfitting. He

9

prefers to save his breath for giving thanks to God. You know well that every adulterer and impure person and lustful man (whose sin really amounts to idolatry) is excluded from the Kingdom of Christ and of God. Do not be deceived by those who make light of impurity. That is the reason why the wrath of God descends on the Pagans. Don't be mixed up with them. Formerly you shared their darkness but now you have become all light in the Lord. Behave then as if light were your very nature. Thus you will produce the fruits proper to light, that is to say every kind of goodness, righteousness and truth. Verify in your own experience that this is what pleases God. Don't participate in any deeds of darkness, which produce no fruit at all. It is better to expose that kind of conduct, although you will be ashamed even to mention such secret vileness. When you do expose such things you let in the light on them and they are changed. Light is the great revealer, and what is revealed by it partakes of its nature. That is the point of our baptismal hymn:

> Awake, O sleeper,
> From thy grave arise.
> The light of Christ upon thee shines.

[15] Look carefully to your steps and tread no heedless ways. We need wise men to seize every opportunity in these evil times. so don't be thoughtless but aim at understanding the Lord's will. Don't give way to intemperance, for it leads to dissoluteness; but fill yourselves with the Spirit. To imbibe Him will give you the kind of joy that expresses itself naturally in our antiphonal chanting of psalms and hymns and songs of the spiritual life, a light-heartedness of voice and music in the Lord, a universal thanksgiving in the name of our Lord Jesus Christ to our God and Father. In that kind of music everyone keeps his place and subordinates himself to the rest out of reverence for Christ.

A Table of Social Duties, or Moral Code

[22] This characteristic of our sacred song should repeat itself in social life.

Wives should subordinate themselves to their husbands as to

the Lord. For the husband is the head and protector of the wife as Christ is the head and saviour of His Body the Church. As the Church is subordinate to Christ, so wives should be subordinate in every way to their husbands.

Husbands should show the same kind of love for their wives as Christ showed for the Church. He gave Himself up to death on her behalf that He might cleanse and consecrate her by means of the bridal bath and vow of Baptism. Thus He could present her to Himself in all her glorious beauty, without any spot of disfigurement or wrinkle of age or any such thing, but entirely holy and blameless. That is how husbands ought to love their wives—as part of themselves. He who loves his wife loves himself. No one ever yet hated his own flesh, but rather we all nourish it and cherish it. So does Christ the Church, for we are limbs of His Body. 'For this reason shall a man leave his father and mother and cling to his wife, and the two of them shall be one flesh.' This analogy of Christ and His Church is far-reaching, and I cannot pursue it further now. However I hope that every one of you will love his wife as he loves himself. And let the wife see that she respect her husband.

VI

Children, obey your parents in the Lord. That is the right thing to do. So says the Commandment, 'Honour thy father and thy mother.' That, by the way, is the first commandment to contain a promise, which runs in effect: 'if you do so, all will go well with you and you will enjoy long life on the earth.'

[4] Fathers, be careful not to exasperate your children. At the same time don't neglect godly discipline and warning.

[5] Slaves should obey their masters with fear and trembling and with such whole-hearted devotion as we offer to Christ Himself. Don't do your work just to catch the eye of your master. As slaves of Christ doing the will of God put your heart into it, and render willing service to your divine Lord rather than to your earthly owner. You know that everyone, whether slave or free,

doing good service, will receive from the Lord an adequate reward.

[9] Masters should adopt a corresponding attitude towards their slaves. Refrain from threatening. Remember that there is in Heaven One who is both their Master and yours. With Him there is no favouritism.

[10] For the rest let all alike realize the strength they possess in the Lord and in the power of His might. Arm yourselves with the full equipment that God has provided to enable His soldiers to hold their own against the tactics of the Devil. We need it all, for our contest is not against flesh and blood but against demonic rulers, potentates, dictators of this dark age, forces of evil in the spiritual sphere. Therefore take the whole divine equipment, which will enable you to maintain your stand in the evil day and to remain victorious on the field of battle. Let truth be your girdle, your breastplate righteousness and your sandals the quick gospel of peace. So take your stand, holding before you the long shield of faith with which to smother all the incendiary missiles hurled at you by the enemy. To protect your head you must wear the helmet of salvation; and your right hand must grasp the sword of the Spirit, which is the word of God. Keep your watch with continuous prayer and supplication, praying the whole time in the Spirit. With constant wakefulness and perseverance you will find opportunity to pray for all the Christian brethren. And please say a special prayer for me, that I may have readiness of speech and boldness of address to make known that mystery which is the essence of the Gospel, and of which I am still the accredited representative although a prisoner in chains. Pray for me then that I may speak with the boldness that my task demands.

Conclusion

[21] In order that you, as well as the others to whom I have written, may know how I am getting on, Tychicus, my dear brother and a faithful Christian minister, will bring you all the news. That is why I am sending him to you, that he may tell

you everything about us. I am sure his news will give you ground for encouragement.

[23] May God our Father and the Lord Jesus Christ grant peace to the Brethren and love with faith. Grace be to all those who love our Lord Jesus Christ with undying constancy.

Philemon

This most human little letter is the only example we have of Paul's unofficial correspondence. Together with the two last letters, it was carried from Rome by Tychicus and the slave Onesimus. The latter must often have wondered how it would be received, for it was addressed to the master whom he had robbed and from whom he had run away.

S. Paul's Letter To Philemon

My dear Colleague,

I am writing to you from prison, where, in company with Timothy, one of our members, I have landed as the result of serving our common Master. We unite in sending greetings to you and to Sister Apphia. Please remember us to Archippus, who has stood shoulder to shoulder with us in many struggles; and also to all the congregation that meets in your house. We pray that God will grant you His help and peace in Christ.

I never forget to mention you in my prayers. And I often find myself thanking God for the love and loyalty that you show to the Lord Jesus and to all the Christian brethren. In doing so, I add a prayer for the brothers themselves that they may share in your loyalty to such an extent as to realize all the benefits that flow from our Christian profession.

I have been especially encouraged lately, my dear brother, by the thought of your love and generosity, for you have relieved our brothers of many anxieties. Consequently, there is no need for me to urge you to do your bounden duty in the particular matter about which I am writing; though I should be quite brave enough in Christ to do that if necessary. But I would much rather appeal to your love for me, an old man and a prisoner for the cause of Christ.

I want to enlist your sympathy on behalf of a convert I have made here in prison—a veritable son born to me while in chains. It is none other than Onesimus. Formerly, I know, he proved a disappointment to you, but now he is a great credit both to you and to me. I am sending him back to you with as much affection as if he were a bit out of my own heart.

I would much rather have kept him here so that he could attend upon me in this prison to which my preaching of the Gospel has brought me. But I was not willing to do that without knowing you would fully approve. I did not want you to confer a favour upon me involuntarily, but of your own free will!

It may be that you lost him for a short time, just in order that you might possess him for ever; though not now as a slave, but as a beloved brother. You can guess how much I love him, but you ought to love him much more, both for his own sake and also because he has entered the service of a fresh Master who is also yours.

I know you look on me as a friend. Very well then, receive him as you would myself. If he did you any injury, such as absconding with your money, I will be your debtor to that extent. (This is a business matter, a formal I.O.U. I write it and sign it with my own hand. I, Paul, will pay the amount in full.)

I need not remind you that as a matter of fact you owe me far more than this—even your own hope of salvation. I should be glad, dear brother, to receive something from you by way of repayment. So do satisfy this most Christian desire of mine. I write in the fullest confidence, knowing you will do even more than I ask.

And by the way, please get ready a spare room for me. I hope that in answer to your prayers I shall soon be with you again.

Epaphras, who has fought so nobly on our side and on Christ's, sends greetings. So also do the others who are working with me, Mark, Aristarchus, Demas and Luke.

With my prayers that Christ's grace may be with you,

Paul

Philippians

Philippi was the first European town in which S. Paul established a church. It was here that he lodged with Lydia, the cloth dyer, on his Second Missionary Journey; here that, after calming the Pythoness or soothsayer and making her useless to her masters, he was with Silas unlawfully flogged; and here that after an earthquake they were released from prison by the frightened magistrates.

Paul's converts in this town seem to have been mostly Pagans, and they never ceased to feel for him the closest affection. Time and again they sent him financial help, and he was more willing to accept it from them than from the rest of his converts. This spirit of mutual confidence pervades the whole letter. Although he still writes with asperity of those who try to insist on circumcision and of those who twist his doctrine of free grace into neglect of the moral law, the only fault he has to find with the Philippians themselves is that they are inclined to be jealous of each other. For the rest, he is full of thanks to them and of gratitude to God.

This is the last of the letters written by S. Paul during his first imprisonment in Rome.

S. Paul's Letter To The Philippians

I

To the Bishop and Deacons and faithful Christians at Philippi.

I, Paul, and Timothy with me, two slaves of Christ Jesus, send greetings and wish you grace and peace from God our Father and the Lord Jesus Christ.

An Expression of Thanks

[3] Every time I think of you my heart leaps with thankfulness to God; and all my prayers are flooded with joy when I remember the good fellowship we have had together in the Gospel from the moment of your conversion until now. And I rejoice also in the confident expectation that He who has begun His good work in you will carry it on to perfection against the day of Christ's appearing.

[7] Of course it is natural for me to think like that about you all, because it is impressed on my mind how helpful you have all been to me both in my imprisonment and in my efforts to defend and maintain the Gospel. I remember, too, how you have all shared with me not only in these things, but also in the Grace of God. God knows that I long after you all with the affection of Christ Himself. This then is my prayer, that your love may grow richer and richer in knowledge and in every kind of perception so that you may give your approval only to the best things. Thus you will be perfect and confident in the day of Christ's coming. And so you will yield the full harvest of righteousness, which comes through Jesus Christ, to the glory and praise of God.

All is well with the Gospel

[12] I should like you to know, my brothers, that my present plight has actually worked out to the advantage of the Gospel. Everyone in the Pretorian Guard and elsewhere knows that I

have been put in prison because I am a Christian. The consequence is that the majority of the brethren have acquired confidence from my chains and are becoming quite fearless in preaching the word of God. There are some indeed who draw public attention to Christ in order to stir up hatred and strife, but others do it genuinely from good will. The latter do it out of love for me, knowing that I am appointed to defend the Gospel; the former proclaim Christ in the spirit of partisans without true sincerity, expecting to make my chains gall me the more. But what does that mean? Only that in every way, whether as a mere pretext or out of sheer honesty, Christ is proclaimed. And for that I am glad.

[19] Yes, and I shall remain glad, for I know that the outcome of all this will be my salvation through your prayers and through a plentiful supply of the Spirit of Jesus Christ. It is my confident assurance that I shall be in no way let down, but that now as always by my complete boldness of speech I shall do honour to Christ in my own person whether by life or by death. To me indeed life means Christ, and death would bring an added advantage. But so long as physical existence gives an opportunity of fruitful work, I hardly know which to prefer. I am on the horns of a dilemma. My own inclination is to set off and be with Christ, which is far the more desirable alternative, but on your account the balance of obligation is to remain at work here. Just because I am sure of this I know that I shall still live and shall remain with you to help forward your progress, and to increase your happiness in the faith. So you need put no restraint on your jubilation in Christ Jesus on my account, for I shall be with you once again.

Lift up your Hearts

[27] There is just one thing—take care to conduct yourselves as good followers of the Gospel of Christ. Whether I come and see you or remain absent and only learn about you from hearsay, be sure to maintain your position in a united spirit, struggling together as one man for the fruit of the Gospel. Do not be in the least degree scared of your adversaries. Such defiance will be for

them an omen of final defeat, but for you of salvation, an omen
sent by God Himself. To you has been granted a great honour,
not only to believe in Christ, but also to suffer on His behalf. Thus
you share the same contest in which you once saw me engaged
and in which you now hear me to be still occupied.

II

Plea for Peace

You have had a rich experience of the comfort given by Christ,
of the persuasive influence of love, of the mutual fellowship
engendered by the Spirit, of every impulse of mercy and pity.
By the recollection of this experience I implore you to be united
in counsel, in sympathy, in purpose; to free yourselves of envy
and of vanity; to think of others in all humility as better than
yourselves; to refrain from pushing your own interests, but
instead to further the interests of others. So will you fill my cup
of gladness to the full. Cultivate the same humility as charac-
terized Christ Jesus. Although He shared the condition of God,
He did not think equality with God a prerogative to be tightly
clutched, but laid aside His divine glory, and, assuming human
likeness, took upon Him the condition of a slave. Thus He
appeared as a man among men, and conducted Himself with
great humility, and carried obedience even to the point of giving
up His life—and that by a malefactor's death upon the cross. As
compensation for such humiliation God has ennobled Him and
given Him a title above all others, so that at the mere mention of
it every living being in the whole universe, whether in Heaven,
on earth or in hell, must do humble reverence, and publicly
proclaim 'Jesus Christ is Lord' to the glory of God the Father.

[12] Beloved, you have always carried out my suggestions when
I have been with you. So I hope that now even more in my
absence you will do what I say and work hard for your own
salvation with meticulous reverence. You have the incentive of
knowing it is God Himself who exercises a benign influence
within you and enables you both to desire and to accomplish the
best purposes. Do everything without complaint or argument.

So you will be blameless and innocent, 'Children of God without blemish in a crooked and perverse generation'. Among such you appear as stars in the firmament of Heaven. Hold fast the word of life, and you will be a credit to me in the Day of Christ, showing that I have not run my course in vain and toiled to no purpose. Even if my own life is to be added to the sacrifice which your faith offers as its due service to God, I am quite happy about it and congratulate you. Do you also be happy about it and congratulate me.

Timothy's proposed Visit

[19] I am hopeful soon, if it is the Lord's will, to send Timothy to you. I need cheering up a little and it will be nice to get his news of you. There is no one else like him at hand who would take so lively an interest in your welfare. People generally pursue their own interests, not those of Christ Jesus. But you know his worth. He has been like a son to me, struggling by my side in the business of the Gospel.

Well, he it is whom I hope to send as soon as I can see what my own fate is to be. But I have confidence in the Lord that He will enable me shortly to come to you myself.

The Return of Epaphroditus

[25] In spite of this I thought it necessary to send Epahproditus back to you at once. He, of course, has been your 'Apostle', sent by you to minister to my needs. To me he has been a brother, a colleague, a fellow-campaigner. He has been longing to see you all and has been very worried since you heard that he was sick. He was indeed very ill, so ill that he nearly died. But God had pity on him, and not on him only, but also on me, so that I should not have to bear a fresh burden of sorrow. The more gladly therefore have I sent him, in order that seeing him again you may take fresh heart of grace, and that in sympathy with you I myself may be less troubled. Give him a cordial Christian welcome. You should honour men like him: he nearly died in doing the work of Christ, and risked his life to render me the services you could not be here to perform.

III

Conclusion

Well, brothers, good-bye, and good cheer. Forgive me if in conclusion I touch on a well-worn topic. It comes easily to me and it may prove salutary for you.

The Judaisers

[2] Be on your guard against those shameless creatures, those mischief-makers, those mutilators of the flesh who insist on circumcision. We are the true 'circumcision' who serve by the Spirit of God, putting our pride in Christ Jesus and not trusting in externals. Although as a matter of fact I of all men might have some reason to trust in externals. If anyone has any reason for that kind of confidence, surely I have. In my case, nothing has been omitted that could constitute a claim on divine favour. I was circumcised on the eighth day; I am a Jew by birth, belonging to the most select tribe of Benjamin; I am a Hebrew of the Hebrews; in observance of the Law I am a Pharisee; I showed my zeal by actually taking the lead in a persecution of the Church; in keeping the requirements of the Law I was blameless.

[7] But all these material advantages I have gladly forfeited for the sake of Christ. And I would gladly forfeit everything I possess for the supreme joy of knowing Christ Jesus my Lord. For Him indeed everything is already forfeit, and I count it all no better than refuse so long as I may gain Christ and be found in Him. In that blissful condition I shall not want to possess any legal righteousness of my own, but only that which comes from trust in Christ, the righteousness given by God in response to faith. That means having personal knowledge of Christ, which comes through experience of the power of His resurrection; and that, of course, involves fellowship with Him in His sufferings. I will gladly have my own nature changed to conform to His death, if only I may somehow attain to the resurrection from the dead.

[12] I don't claim that I have already attained it, or that I have already reached the state of perfection, but I press forward

to grasp it, knowing well that I have already been myself grasped by Christ Jesus. I don't mean by that, brothers, that the prize is already in my grasp. I only assert this one thing, that refusing to look behind and straining breast-forward towards the goal, I press on to win the prize of Heaven, to which God has called me in Christ Jesus.

[15] This surely is the only right attitude of mind for all mature Christians. But if any of you fail to see it in this light, I feel sure that God will reveal it to you. Only we must be careful to walk by the light we have.

The Antinomians

[17] In present circumstances the only safe course for you, my brothers, is to get together and become imitators of me. Keep under close observation those who follow our pattern of life and take us as your practical standard. For there are many of whose conduct I have often warned you and now remind you with tears. They are altogether hostile to the teaching of the Cross with its implication of self-sacrifice. They are destined for perdition; gluttony is their god; shame is their pride; their thoughts are centred in material things. We, on the other hand, are colonists from Heaven, and our conduct conforms to that fact. From there we expect the arrival of our deliverer, the Lord Jesus Christ. He will change this humble body of ours and make it like His own glorious body, through the exercise of that mighty power which enables Him to subdue the whole universe to His will.

IV

Final Advice

Well, my brothers, you whom I so dearly love and so long to see, you who are my joy and crown, take care, dear brothers, that you stand fast in the Lord. I hope that Euodias and Syntyche will settle their differences and live at peace with one another in the Lord. And I would ask you, my good colleague, to assist them to this end, for they struggled by my side on behalf of the Gospel in the early days with Clement and the rest of my assistants whose names are now written in the Book of Life.

[4] Never let yourselves be downhearted, but always keep up your spirits in the Lord. Let everyone see how gentle and forbearing you are. The Lord's coming is very near. Don't be over-anxious about anything, but in every case make your needs known to God by prayer and supplication, remembering to thank Him for all He has done. And the peace of God, which passes all human understanding, will keep watch and ward over your hearts and thoughts in Christ Jesus.

[8] For the rest, my brethren, let your minds dwell on such things as truth, holiness, justice, purity, loveliness, honour, and on every kind of excellence and merit. Put into practice all that you have ever learnt or heard or received or know from me. Thus will the God of peace remain with you.

[10] I am very glad to know that concern on my behalf had once again begun to exercise your minds. I don't mean to imply that you were not thinking of me all the time, but that there was nothing you could do. In any case I am not complaining of actual need, for by this time I have learned to be content in any circumstances. I can live in the humblest condition as well as in the midst of plenty. I have been initiated into the art of living in in every kind of situation, feasting and hunger, famine and abundance. I can support them all through Him who gives me strength. But I am very grateful to you for your practical sympathy with me in my affliction.

[15] You Philippians know better than anyone that at the beginning of my gospel preaching, when I left Macedonia, there was no question of giving or receiving money between me and any other church except yourselves. But you, even when I was at Thessalonica, sent two or three times to supply my needs. Not that I want the gift, but I do want to see the interest accruing from your bounty mount up on your side of the account. I am fully paid up and more. I am indeed overwhelmed by the present you sent through Epaphroditus. That is a fragrant and acceptable sacrifice; which must give much pleasure to God. I am sure

that God on my behalf will satisfy all your needs out of the treasure of His glory in Christ Jesus. To God our Father be glory for ever and ever. Amen.

[21] Give my greetings to every Christian brother. The brethren who are with me send their best wishes. All our Church members send greetings, including those who belong to the staff of the Imperial household.

The grace of our Lord Jesus Christ be with your spirit.

The Pastorals

The three letters grouped under this head are so called because they give instructions to the Pastors, Timothy and Titus, about the exercise of their office. Inevitably they deal with matters of ecclesiastical organisation. Many modern scholars think that the picture here given of that organisation is too developed for the lifetime of S. Paul. They find their doubt increased by the presence of many words not found elsewhere in the Pauline writings. They therefore conclude that the letters, although containing material by S. Paul, were actually composed by some later writer.

This is the fashionable view in the learned world to-day, but it is not necessarily correct. A sufficient explanation of the difficulties may be found if it can be agreed that S. Paul's life was prolonged beyond the period of his imprisonment at Rome. He was probably released and then resumed his missionary labours until he was again taken into custody and brought back to Rome to suffer martyrdom. In that case, the letters would have as their background this final period of the Apostle's life, a period not disclosed in the Acts of the Apostles, which end with S. Paul still undergoing his first Roman imprisonment.

A reasonable reconstruction of the history would be as follows: After his release the Apostle fulfilled his ambition to see Spain. But presently he took up again his old work at Ephesus. On a temporary absence on a journey to Macedonia and elsewhere, he left Timothy behind to guard the purity of Christian teaching, and while still travelling wrote to give him the instructions contained in I Timothy. On this journey he visited Crete, and on his departure from the island left Titus to complete the ecclesiastical organisation, which he himself had left in a somewhat embryonic state. His instructions were reduced to writing and were conveyed to Titus in the epistle that bears his name. Later—how much later we do not know—Paul was again taken prisoner, and from Rome he wrote once more to Timothy giving him final instructions and inviting him to rejoin him at the earliest possible moment.

S. Paul's First Letter To Timothy

I

From Paul, appointed an Apostle of Christ Jesus by command of God our saviour and of Christ Himself, in whom rests our hope, to Timothy.

My true son in the faith,

May God our Father and Christ Jesus our Lord bestow upon you grace, mercy and peace.

Timothy's Task

When I moved on to Macedonia I asked you to stay behind in Ephesus in order that you might warn certain of your friends to abstain from teaching novelties, and to avoid superstitious fables and limitless genealogies; for they rather provide questions for discussion than further the task of the sacred ministry, which must be performed in faith. I should like to remind you of that duty again now. The aim of our teaching is love, flowing from a pure heart, a clear conscience and single-minded loyalty. Some of our people have failed through deserting these virtues for futile arguments in a desire to make themselves 'Rabbis' or teachers of the Law. But they succeed in understanding neither the statements they make nor the explanations they so stoutly affirm.

[8] We know that the Law is sound if a teacher interprets it in a legitimate way, recognizing that it is not enacted for the law-abiding but for all the others—the lawless and insubordinate, the impious and the sinners, the irreverent and profane, the slayers of father or mother and other murderers, the adulterers and pederasts, the kidnappers, liars and perjurers, and every kind of person who rebels against sound teaching which is in accordance with that glorious gospel of God most blessed wherewith I was entrusted.

[12]   I offer special thanks to our Lord Jesus Christ, to whom I owe my present position, because He thought me sufficiently trustworthy to put me into the ministry, although I was once a blasphemer and assailant and persecutor of the Church. But I was shown mercy because I did it in the ignorance of unbelief. Our Lord overwhelmed me with His favour and supplied me freely with the faith and love that are peculiarly His. Truly it is a reliable saying and worthy of special credence: 'Christ Jesus came into the world to save sinners.' I am myself a supreme sinner. Yet I was shown mercy for this reason—that in me particularly Jesus Christ might show the full extent of His forbearance, and that I might become an example of those who through faith in Him should attain eternal life. To God alone, incorruptible, invisible, Lord of Eternity, belong honour and glory for ever and ever. Amen.

[18]   These instructions I lay upon you, son Timothy, in accordance with what was said by the prophets who recommended you to me for the ministry. Conduct your campaign on these lines and it will be successful. Preserve a loyal faith and a good conscience. Some have forfeited the latter and have wrecked their whole faith. Among them I number Hymenaeus and Alexander, whom I have excommunicated. They must learn not to blaspheme.

II

Public Prayer

First then I bid you see that supplication, prayer, petitions and thanksgiving, be offered for all sorts of men, especially for sovereign rulers and for all in authority, that we may live a quiet and peaceable life with all piety and dignity. That will be good in itself and will be pleasing to God our Saviour, for He desires that every one should be saved and come to the knowledge of the truth. There is one God and one intermediary between God and man, the man Jesus Christ, who gave Himself a ransom for all. That was the culmination of God's revelation appropriate to this age. Of it I was appointed the official herald and representative.

(I am speaking the literal truth without any prevarication.) I was appointed to instruct the Pagans in faith and truth.

[9] My wish then is that at every meeting the men shall be responsible for leading the prayers—lifting up holy hands with complete freedom from jealousy and disputes. It is of equal importance to see that the women dress quietly, with modesty and moderation—not with elaborate coiffures and gold and pearls and expensive costumes. But, as befits women who make a profession of religion, let their adornment be that of kind deeds. A woman's duty is to show herself a quiet and submissive learner. I do not allow women to take office as teachers, or to have the direction of men; theirs is a silent service. We can learn this from the order of nature. Adam was created first and then Eve. And it was not Adam who was deceived, but his wife was deceived and yielded to temptation. However the evil will be remedied and women will obtain salvation through their child-bearing, if they continue faithful, loving, holy and modest.

III

Rules for Appointment of Ministry

It is truly said that he who aspires to be a bishop aims at an excellent office. A bishop has to be irreproachable, with only one wife, a moderate man, temperate, genial, hospitable, a skilled teacher, not too fond of wine, or too ready with a blow, but gentle and conciliatory, a good manager in his own house, and one who brings up his children to be obedient and respectful. If a man does not know how to manage his own household, how can he take charge of a church of God? He should not be a recent convert, or he may be blinded by conceit and lay himself open to much criticism. He should be in good repute with those out-side the Church, so that if any unjust slander is started against him he may have a chance of escaping the trap set by his accuser.

[8] Similarly Deacons should be men of respect in the com-munity, straightforward in speech, not addicted to drink, not avaricious, holding the revealed faith with a clear conscience. Let such be first put on probation; then if no objection is alleged

against them they can take up their office. Their wives too must be worthy of respect, no scandalmongers, but temperate and in every way dependable. The Deacon must have only one wife, and he must be a good manager of children and of his own home. Those who do well in this ministry make a good standing for themselves and acquire boldness in proclaiming the Christian faith.

[14] I send you these instructions in the expectation that I shall shortly be with you. If I am delayed they will give you the necessary information for carrying on the arrangements of God's household. That is what a church of the living God really is, a pillar and foundation to uphold the Truth. And who does not agree how profound is the revealed truth of our religion? As the hymn on the Incarnation tells us:

> First in our flesh as God made known,
> Then in the spirit guileless proved,
> The angels preached Him to the world,
> And Heaven received the accepted Lord.

IV

A Warning

The Spirit has told us in so many words that in the Last Days some will apostatize from the faith and attach themselves to spiritual errors and demoniacal doctrines, taught by specious liars who are branded as such in their own conscience. They will prohibit marriage, and they will order people to abstain from certain kinds of food, which God has created to be received thankfully by the faithful and such as know the truth. Everything created by God is good, and nothing is to be forbidden, provided it is received with thanksgiving, for then it is consecrated not only by God's word at the creation but also by the grace said over it.

Personal Advice to Timothy with regard to his own Conduct

[6] Keep this point of view before the brethren, and you will show yourself a good minister of Christ Jesus, thoroughly versed in the formulas of the faith and of the sound doctrine that you

have already followed. Don't let yourself be taken up with irreligious, old-womanish fables. Religion is a matter of serious training. Exercise of the body has a certain value, but religion is of universal service, holding as it does a promise of life both here and hereafter. That is a reliable statement and worthy of universal acceptance. Such is the end for which we toil and struggle, because we have put our hope in a living God, who is the Saviour of all men, particularly of the faithful.

[11] Make these points the subject of your instruction and teaching. Don't give anyone reason to look down upon you for your youth and inexperience, but set a good example to all the converts in speech, behaviour, love, faith and holiness. While awaiting my arrival give special attention to the public reading of the Scriptures, to preaching and to teaching. Don't forget to use the grace you actually possess, which was given you when, after consulting the prophets, the presbyters laid their hands upon your head. Pay attention to these things; give yourself wholly to them, and then your progress will be obvious to all. Be careful not to make any slip either in your behaviour or in your teaching. Stick to your job. By so doing you will serve both yourself and those who listen to you.

V

How to deal with Various Classes

Never minister a rebuke to an elderly man, but rather appeal to him as a father. With the younger men you can deal as brothers, the elder women as mothers, the younger as sisters, with due regard to the proprieties.

Widows who are destitute must be treated with respect and given assistance. But if a widow has children or grandchildren they should be taught that the first duty of religious people is to their own home and that they must make some return to those who were responsible for their upbringing. That is the kind of conduct that will win the approbation of God. She who in her widowhood is left utterly bereft fixes her hope on God and spends her time in supplications and prayers night and day. But the

widow who gives herself up to dissipation is no better than a
living corpse. You had better issue instructions so that all may
avoid reproach. If anyone fails to make provision for his relatives
and especially those of his own immediate family, he is a traitor
to the faith and worse than one who has never embraced it. Let
no widow be enrolled on the formal list under sixty years of age.
She must have been only once married. She must have a good
reputation as a worker, one who has brought up children, has
been hospitable, ready to offer personal service, kind to the dis-
tressed, given to all sorts of good works. That is the type of widow
to enrol. But don't take on young widows. For if passion replace
their love for Christ they want to marry, and then they are condemned for having lost their first faith. Besides they cultivate
idleness as a profession; they gad about from house to house and
become not only idlers but gossipers and busybodies, retailers of
petty scandal. So I prefer the younger widows to marry, keep
house and bear a family. Then they will give our opponents no
excuse to bring charges against us. Already we have had some
who have fallen away to Satan. If therefore any of our members
have widows dependent upon them they must look after them,
and not let the Church be burdened with them. That will give
the Church an opportunity to look after those who are really
destitute.

[17] Presbyters who have shown themselves good administrators
should be deemed worthy of additional stipend, especially those
who have also shown themselves efficient in preaching and teaching. The Bible says 'Thou shalt not muzzle the ox that treadeth
out the corn'; and 'The workman deserves his wages'. Do not
entertain a charge against a Presbyter unless it is supported by
the evidence of two or three witnesses. Those who have committed definite sin you must reprimand publicly, as a warning to
the rest. I charge you most solemnly, before God and Christ
Jesus and the chosen angels, to observe these instructions without
prejudice and without partiality. Ordain no man without due
preparation, or you may appear to condone the sins of an un-
worthy candidate, and so to share them. Take care that there
are no gross sins in your own life. But you need no longer be a
total abstainer. I think you ought to take a little wine for the

sake of your digestion and to strengthen you against your frequent bouts of sickness. Some men's sins are open and cry aloud for condemnation, but in other cases they are less obvious and require to be brought to notice. Similarly some good deeds are known to all; and even the more hidden sort cannot long be concealed.

VI

Moral Code

Servants who are slaves must remember to regard their masters as entitled to all proper respect. Otherwise the name of God and the Christian teaching may be brought into disrepute. Those who belong to Christian masters must not look down upon them because from the religious point of view they are only brothers, but they must render all the better service because those who receive the benefit of that service are friends and fellow-believers.

[3] Make all this the subject of your teaching and preaching. If anyone teaches the contrary or quarrels with sound doctrine (which is that of our Lord Jesus Christ) and with your pious instruction, then he is an ignoramus blinded by self-conceit. Such men dote upon finicking quotations and controversies, out of which you get nothing but bad feeling, quarrels, insults, injurious insinuations, and constant friction—the characteristic traits of people with perverted minds and strangers to the truth, who combine religion with self-interest. (And of course religion does comport with true self-interest when it is coupled with a contented mind.) As we brought nothing with us into this world, so it is certain we can carry nothing out. If then, we have food and clothes, that ought to be enough. Those who want to get rich are caught in the snare of temptation and develop many unreasonable and harmful tastes, which ultimately land them in ruin and destruction. Love of money is a source of every kind of evil. Some who have grasped at it have wandered from the faith and have suffered much distress of mind.

[11] But you, servant of God, must avoid this kind of thing. Make your aim righteousness, piety, faith, love, patience, gentleness. So wage the great contest of the faith that you win the

crown of eternal life. To that life you were called in your baptism, when in the presence of many witnesses you made public profession of a sound belief. Most solemnly do I urge you before God, the author of all life, and Christ Jesus, who made good His profession in the court of Pontius Pilate, keep the charge then laid upon you free from stain and reproach until the appearance of our Lord Jesus Christ. At the right moment He will be revealed by the blessed and only Potentate, King of Kings and Lord of Lords, who is the sole fount of immortality, the dweller in light inaccessible, whom no mortal eye has seen or can ever see. To Him be honour and power for ever. Amen.

[17] Advise those who are rich in this world's goods not to think themselves superior. Let them not pin their hope on such transient wealth but rather upon God who is the provider of all riches for our enjoyment. Tell them to lead useful lives, to be rich in kind deeds, generous, ready to share with others, laying a good foundation of solid wealth for the future that they may maintain a firm grasp of the life that is life indeed.

[20] Guard well, my dear Timothy, the traditional faith. Have nothing to do with the meaningless jargon and the nice distinctions of esoteric 'Wisdom'. By making that profession some have completely missed the mark of faith. Grace be with you.

A Second Letter To Timothy

I

To Timothy from Paul, one of the Apostles of Christ Jesus, commissioned by God to proclaim that new life which He has promised in Christ Jesus.

My dear Son,
   Grace, mercy and peace be yours from God our Father and Christ Jesus our Lord.

[3] I thank God, the God of our fathers, whom I also continue to worship with a clear conscience, that I never for one moment allow the thought of you to drop out of my prayers. Night and day I long to see you, for I still remember the tears you shed at our parting. And I am filled with joy at being reminded of your sincere faith—a faith that was first evident in your grandmother, Lois, and then in your mother, Eunice, and now, I know full well, is possessed by you also.

Advice on Ministerial Conduct

[6] Just because you carry on this tradition of faith I want to remind you to stir into living flame the divine gift which was transmitted to you by the laying on of my hands. God did not give us a spirit of timidity, but of power and love and self-control. Do not then display any diffidence in witnessing on behalf of our Lord or in acknowledging your relation to me His prisoner. Bear all the suffering that attends the preaching of the Gospel in the power of God, who first saved us and then called us to this sacred vocation. This He did, not for any special desert of ours, but purely out of His own gracious purpose, which He formed for us in Christ Jesus before the beginning of time, and has now made clear in the appearance of our Saviour Jesus Christ. He has annihilated death and poured a flood of new light on life and immortality by means of the Gospel.

[11] Of that Gospel I have been appointed a preacher and an Apostle and a teacher. That is the reason why I endure these misfortunes. But I am not ashamed of it, for I know in whom I have believed and I am certain that He is able to keep what I have deposited with Him against the Last Day.

[13] As an example of wholesome doctrine, take the teaching you received from me, which was indeed inspired by the faith and love we learn from Christ Jesus. The good tradition deposited with us you must guard by the Holy Spirit who has taken up His abode in us.

[15] You have heard already that in Rome all our Asiatic Christians have carefully avoided me, including Phygellus and Hermogenes. May the Lord grant special mercy to the members of Onesiphorus' household, for he often cheered me up and was not ashamed of me even though I was a prisoner. When he was in Rome he looked for me everywhere until he found me. May he find mercy of the Lord at the last Day. What great service he rendered me in Ephesus you are already aware from personal knowledge.

II

The Ministry demands Strength

Do you then, my son, shew yourself strong in the grace derived from Christ Jesus. The instructions I have given you in the presence of many witnesses must be handed on to faithful men who will be able, in their turn, to teach others. Endure your share of hardship like a good soldier of Christ Jesus. No one who has joined the army ties himself up with civilian business or he may fall foul of his commanding officer. And no athlete can expect to win a prize if he does not keep the rules of the contest. Similarly, the farmer who sticks to his job will be the first to benefit from the harvest. Be sure you catch my meaning. I have no doubt the Lord will make you quick to grasp the significance of all sorts of questions.

[8] Keep in mind the phrases: 'Jesus Christ, descended from David, raised from the dead.' That is the Gospel I preach. For it I suffer the indignity of chains on the charge that I am a

flagitious person. But no chains can bind the Word of God.
Therefore, I put up with every kind of suffering for the sake of
the Elect, in order that they may win the final salvation which is
to be found in Christ Jesus with eternal glory. Truly is it said
in our Martyrs' Hymn:

> Die we with Christ,
>   And we shall live with Him:
> Endure all,
>   And with Him we shall reign.
>
> Deny we Him,
>   Ourselves shall be denied—
> But seek His love
>   'Twill hold in spite of all.
>
> Dim though our faith,
>   The Christ will faithful prove.
> We are in Him:
>   Himself He cannot fail.

[14] Remind your people of this. Instruct them solemnly
before God not to waste time in battles about words, which are
no good to anybody, but only upset the listeners. Try to make
yourself approved by God, a workman who has no need to be
ashamed of his work, but gives well proportioned teaching on the
word of truth. Avoid all empty discussions, which only lead to
irreverence. Such arguments spread corruption like a gangrenous
wound. Among those who take part in them are Hymenaeus and
Philetus, men who have missed the mark of truth and affirm that
the resurrection is over and gone already. They have succeeded
in upsetting the faith of a certain number. However, the Church
so firmly founded by God still stands and the inscriptions on its
foundation-stone are still intact: 'The Lord knows His own' and
'Everyone who invokes the name of the Lord must abstain from
evil.'

[20] In a great house there are not only gold and silver vessels,
but others of wood and earthenware. Some are both decorative

and useful while others are merely useful. If any one of you manages to keep himself free from those evils I have mentioned, he will be like one of the more decorative vessels, dedicated to the Master's service, which are not only beautiful, but also adapted to all sorts of useful functions.

[22]   Avoid those temptations that are natural to a young man. Cultivate righteousness, faith, love, peace in company with all who call upon the Lord with honest hearts. Don't get involved in silly and ignorant questionings, for they are a fruitful source of controversy. The Lord's servant must not quarrel, but be gentle to all, good at teaching, slow to take offence, one who can reduce his opponents by the mildness of his manners. There is always a chance that God may bring them to a change of mind and lead them to acknowledge the truth. They may thus escape from the devilish snares in which they have been entangled, and be restored again to a sober life to fulfil the purposes of God.

III

Future Troubles

Do realize this, that before the end comes we shall have to pass through very difficult times. Men will be selfish, avaricious, boastful, irreverent, callous, implacable, scurrilous, intemperate, violent, evil-minded, treacherous, reckless, conceited, pleasure-seekers rather than God-seekers, practising the externals of religion while denying its inner power. Avoid all such. Of their number are they who insinuate themselves into people's houses and get hold of such women as are burdened with sins and swayed by all kinds of passions, always ready to listen to some fresh fancy, but never able to grasp any solid truth.

[8]   It was in this way that the Egyptian magicians, Jannes and Jambres, set themselves up in opposition to Moses. Similarly, those of whom I speak oppose the truth, men of depraved mind and utterly worthless when tested by standards of faith. However, they are not likely to make much progress, for their folly will be exposed to everyone, as was that of the magicians in the end.

[10] But you have learnt your lesson from me and my experiences. You have seen my teaching, training, planning, faith, patience, love, fortitude, persecution, sufferings—in fact all that happened to me in Antioch, Iconium and Lystra. You saw what persecutions I had to undergo and know the Lord rescued me from them all. And indeed, all who want to live religious lives in Christ Jesus will have to suffer persecution. Evil persons and impostors will grow worse and worse, deceiving and being deceived. But you must hold fast to the truths you have learnt and to your convictions, remembering who were your teachers. From childhood you have been familiar with the sacred Scriptures. They can impart the wisdom that will assure you salvation through trust in Christ Jesus. Every inspired writing is also valuable for instruction, for the defence of the faith, for edification, for training in righteousness. By its use the man of God may become a finished product, fully equipped for every kind of duty.

IV

Be Diligent

I lay upon you a solemn charge before God and Christ Jesus, who will judge the living and the dead, by His coming and by His Kingdom: Be an insistent preacher of the Word. Press on with that task on every sort of occasion, suitable or unsuitable. Scold and warn and encourage your hearers. Never lose patience and never stop teaching. The time will come when men will refuse to accept sound doctrine, but according to their own ideas they will collect teachers just to tickle their ears. So their attention will be diverted from the truth and they will be inveigled into accepting mere legends. But you must maintain in all circumstances your soberness of judgment. Bear up against difficulties. Do your duty as an evangelist. Serve your ministry to the full.

[6] I am already offering the libation of my own life, and the moment for my deaprture is already here. I have played my part in the great contest; I have run my race; I have preserved my loyalty to the faith. Now I wait to receive the victor's crown of

righteousness, which the Lord will hand to me at the Last Day. And since He is a good umpire, He will award the prize not only to me, but also to all those who have shewn a true desire for His appearing.

Personal Details

[9] Do your best to come to me at once. Demas has left me because he was too attached to this material world. He has gone to Thessalonica. Crescens has departed for Galatia, Titus for Dalmatia. Luke is the only one left with me. Pick up Mark and bring him with you: he will be specially useful to attend on me. Tychicus I have sent to Ephesus. When you come please bring with you the overcoat I left behind in Troas at Carpus' house. Bring the books, too, and don't forget the documents.

[14] Alexander, the coppersmith, has done me much harm. 'According to his deeds, will the Lord deal with him.' You had better beware of him too; he was a bitter opponent of everything I said. At my first cross-examination I had no one to defend me or to vouch for me, but everyone left me severely alone. I hope it will not be brought up against them. But the Lord was with me and strengthened me to give a full statement of the Gospel in the hearing of all the Pagans. So was I rescued from the lion's mouth. The Lord will rescue me from every evil machination and preserve me for His Heavenly Kingdom. His is the glory for ever and ever. Amen.

[19] My kind regards to Priscilla and Aquila and to the family of Onesiphorus. Erastus has stayed in Corinth, and I left Trophimus behind in Miletum sick. Do your best to come before winter sets in. Eubulus sends kind regards and so do Pudens, Linus, Claudia and all the brethren.

[22] The Lord be with your spirit, my dear Timothy, and with you all be grace.

Letter To Titus

I

My true Son in the one Faith,

Grace be yours and peace from God the Father and Christ Jesus our Saviour.

Although I am the merest slave of God I am still an Apostle of Jesus Christ, with a commission to fulfil in respect of that faith which belongs to God's chosen ones and of that religious truth which alone can confer hope of everlasting life. God Himself, who cannot lie, established the promise of such life as part of His eternal purpose; and now at the appropriate season He has revealed it in the message which I have been commissioned to preach by the command of God our Saviour.

Church Officers

[5] This is the reason why I left you behind in Crete, that you might put the final touches on our organization there and appoint presbyters in every town. According to the instructions I gave you, choose men of good reputation, married but with one wife only, whose children have been brought up in the faith and are free from any charge of loose living or insubordination.

[7] The Bishop must be a man of irreproachable character, for he is the steward of God's household. He must be considerate of others' opinions, not easily moved to anger, not addicted to wine, not violent, not venal. He must be hospitable, a promoter of good causes, serious-minded, a just man and good, with complete self-control. He must hold fast to the truths of sound doctrine so that he may be able to inspire comfort and courage through the healthful tone of his discourses and at the same time defeat the arguments of opponents.

False Teachers

[10] There are many who go their own way and talk the emptiest trash, and yet pervert the minds of others. You find

11

them especially amongst the Judaisers, whom you must do your best to reduce to silence. They are perverting whole households by their false teaching, and out of it they are earning a dishonest livelihood. One of their countrymen, a prophet of their own, described them well:

> Cretans always liars were
> Idle gluttons, beasts to fear.

That description is true. Therefore rebuke them sharply. They should develop a healthy faith and not cling to Jewish fables or to ritual enactments coined by men who garble the truth. There is no such thing as ceremonial defilement. The pure can handle anything without being defiled. But to the impure and unbelieving nothing is pure, because they are already defiled in mind and conscience. They claim to know God, but by their acts they repudiate Him; detestable creatures, always 'against the government' but quite useless for any positive good.

II

Moral Code

You on the other hand should inculcate the conduct that goes with sound doctrine. Tell the older men that they must be temperate, dignified, sensible, sound in faith, in love, in perseverance. Similarly the older women should be reverent in behaviour; they must not be scandal-mongers, nor slaves of strong drink, but good counsellors. Thus they will train the young women to love their husbands and their children, to be prudent, chaste, good housewives, submissive to their husbands. Then it will not be possible to bring any charge against the preaching of the Word of God.

[6] Similarly bid the young men to be temperate in every respect. See that you yourself give an example of correct behaviour. In your teaching let there be no flippancy or irreverence. Use sound arguments to which no exception can be taken. Thus our opponents will find nothing evil to say of us and will be confounded.

[9]   Slaves must obey their own masters in all circumstances.
They should set themselves to please; they should not be contra-
dictious; they must not start pilfering; but in everything they
should show genuine loyalty, and so bring universal credit on
the doctrine of God our Saviour.

What to Teach

[11]   To all classes has been vouchsafed the revelation of God's
saving grace, teaching us to repudiate our irreligious lives and
our carnal passions, and to live temperate, just and sober lives in
this present world, while we await the fulfilment of our hope of
blessedness and the unveiling of the glory of our great God and
Saviour Jesus Christ.   He gave Himself on our behalf in order
that He might redeem us from all lawlessness and thus secure
for Himself a people for His own possession, devoted to goodness.
That is what you should teach—authoritatively, with mingled
encouragement and warning.   Don't let anyone have reason to
be supercilious about you.

III

The Good Life

   Remind them that they must submit to ruling authorities—
they must obey the regulations, be ready to share in any good
work, refuse to speak harshly of anyone, be conciliatory and
reasonable, and show complete courtesy to all kinds of people.
We ourselves were once outlaws, rebellious, deceitful, slaves to
various passions and pleasures, spending our lives in malice and
envy, hateful and hating one another.   But then our Saviour God
showed His graciousness and kindness, in that for no righteous
acts done by ourselves but purely out of His own mercy He saved
us through the new birth of Baptism and the new life of the Holy
Spirit.   That Spirit He poured out on us in rich measure through
Jesus Christ our Saviour in order that once we were 'justified'
by His grace we might become inheritors of the hope of eternal
life.

What to Avoid

[8]   The truth of this statement I can thoroughly guarantee, and
I advise you to insist on that aspect of the truth, so that those who

profess belief in God may make up their minds to be forward in good works. Men will find such counsel good and helpful. But avoid trifling arguments, and questions about genealogical trees, and wordy battles about the Law. They are unhelpful and futile. If a factious person remains stubborn after a first and second admonition, have no more to do with him. Clearly such a man is self-condemned and is sinning perversely.

Last Instructions

[12] When I send Artemus or Tychicus to replace you, come to me as soon as you can at Nicopolis, where I have determined to spend the winter. Send Zenas, the lawyer, and Apollos to me at once, and see that they have everything they need. Let our people learn to show themselves forward in kind offices to meet such emergencies, so that they may have something to show for their religion.

All of us here send greetings. Give our best wishes to all our friends in the faith.

Grace be with you all.

James

There is nothing to indicate explicitly which of the three Jameses mentioned in the New Testament is the author of this epistle. But he was most probably the 'brother of the Lord', who came to occupy the position of bishop of the church in Jerusalem and was ultimately put to death by Annas, the High Priest.

James was the leader of the Jewish Christians, with some of whom S. Paul so often found himself at variance. This explains the Old Testament flavour of the composition, although some scholars account for it further by suggesting that S. James wrote it to persuade the unconverted section of the Jewish race. It is more likely, however, that the letter was especially intended for the Jewish Christians in Asia Minor.

The author's method of presenting Christian truth is, of course, quite different from S. Paul's. Note, for instance, the strongly contrasted treatment of Faith. Nevertheless, there are some phrases in Romans which suggest that S. Paul had read James's letter with appreciation (compare Rom. ii. 13 with James i. 22). Indeed, if we bear in mind the frequent protestations against quarrelsomeness, it may seem that the letter was intended to pour oil on troubled waters and to restrain the Jewish Christians from making things too difficult for S. Paul's Gentile converts. It will be noticed, too, that the denunciations of the rich recall the poverty of the Jerusalem Christians to which S. Paul often called attention.

An Open Letter From James

I

James, a servant of God and of His Messiah the Lord Jesus, sends greetings to the members of the Jewish race living in foreign parts.

My Brothers.

Need for Constancy

[2] Do not be worried if you find yourselves subjected to all sorts of trials, but regard them rather as a special privilege, for you know that their purpose is to test your faith, and that such testing makes for perseverance. Only see that you persevere to the end, so that you may attain an entire perfection, in no respect deficient.

[5] If any of you is deficient in wisdom, let him ask of God, who gives to all without grudging or reproach, and his request will be granted. But let him ask in faith, without doubting, for he who doubts is like a sea-wave driven by the wind and tossed every way. Such a man cannot expect to receive anything from the Lord. He is inevitably a man of two minds without any stability of character.

Class Troubles in the Church

[9] Our religion is a great leveller. Therefore let every one of you who is of humble parentage rejoice that he has been raised to a new dignity. By the same token the rich should be glad of his new humility. He should remember that his destined end is to fade away like a prairie flower. The sun is no sooner up with its scorching heat than the grass is dried, the flower is fallen and its beauty is perished. So shall the rich man be cut off in the midst of all his business.

God not the Source of Temptation

[12] Happy then is the man who perseveres in the midst of trials. When he has been tested he will receive the crown of life, which has been promised to those who love God. But don't let anyone say under the process of testing, 'This trial is put upon me by God.' For as God is free from all temptation to evil, He never Himself inflicts it on others. When a man is tempted he is first enticed and seduced by his own desire. Then desire conceives and gives birth to sin. And sin, when it has run its course, issues in death. Don't make any mistake, my dear brothers, it is only good and perfect gifts that come from above. They proceed from the Father of the heavenly constellations. His light never grows dim, and earth's shadows are never caused by any turning or capriciousness on His part. It was His deliberate plan that we should be born again by the word of truth, and that we should be a kind of first fruits from His whole creation. You can be very sure, my dear brothers, that there has been no change in that plan.

Religion is Action

[20] Let everyone be quick to listen, slow to speak, slow to show anger. Human anger does not establish the justice of God. Clear away then all the rank growth of hatred from your hearts and make of gentleness a soil to receive the seedling word, which alone can save your souls. However do not delude yourselves by merely listening to the word, but let your listening bear fruit in action. He who listens to the word and does not act upon it is like a man who has seen his face in a mirror and when he has recognized his reflection goes away and immediately forgets what he looks like. But the man who has gazed upon the perfect law of liberty and keeps the vision of it constantly before him proves himself not one who hears and forgets, but one who listens and obeys. Such a man is happy in everything he undertakes. Conversely if anyone fancies he is religious and keeps no check on his tongue, he deceives himself and renders his religion futile. Religion to prove itself true and uncorrupt in the sight of God our Father must not only keep itself unsoiled by the world but also minister to the needs of the orphan and widow.

II

No Class Distinctions in the Church

My brothers, do not let your presentation of the faith of our gracious Lord Jesus Christ be spoiled by snobbishness. If a man comes into your church wearing jewellery and immaculate clothes, and there comes in also a poor man very down at heel, and when you see the well-dressed man you say to him, 'Sit here, this is one of our best seats,' and you say to the shabby person, 'You can sit here on the floor,' are you not showing partiality and giving evidence of a mean discrimination? Look, my dear brothers, was it not those who are poor in this world's goods that God chose to make rich in faith and heirs of the Kingdom promised to them that love Him? But you have dishonoured the poor. Is it not the rich who have oppressed you and dragged you into court? Do not they pour scorn on the proud name by which you are called? If you fulfil the Royal Law in accordance with the command, 'Thou shalt love thy neighbour as thyself,' your conduct is correct. But if you display partiality, you are committing a sin and are shown up by the Law as transgressors. For an observer of the Law to fail in one article is to be guilty in respect of the whole. For He who said, Thou shalt not commit adultery, said also, Thou shalt not kill. It follows that if you avoid adultery but commit murder, you have become a law-breaker.

[12] See that your profession and your conduct are such as do credit to men who expect to be judged by the law of liberty. Judgment will be passed without mercy on those who show no mercy. But mercy forestalls judgment.

Faith and Works

[14] What good is it, brethren, if a man asserts that he possesses faith but does not reveal it in his actions? Can belief save him? Suppose a brother or sister is short of clothing or deprived of daily food and one of you says to them, 'Good luck to you; keep

warm and be sure you get enough to eat,' but gives them nothing
for their bodily needs, what good is it? So faith, if it does not
issue in act, expires with itself. Someone may well say, 'You have
faith and I have deeds; show me your faith, if you can, without deeds, and I will show you mine by means of my deeds.'
You believe, you say, that there is one God? That's good. The
demons show that amount of faith and are in terror because of
it. Don't you realize, my poor fellow, that faith without action
is an empty husk? Was it not by action that our father Abraham
was justified when he offered his son Isaac upon the altar? Faith,
you see, expresses itself in deeds and was rounded off with
action. That is the true explanation of the Scripture text,
'Abraham believed God and it was reckoned to him for righteousness and he was called "The Friend of God".' So you see a
man is justified by his deeds and not by belief alone.

[25]   Similarly was it not by deeds that the prostitute Rahab
put herself right when she gave shelter to our spies and got them
away by an unguarded road? It follows then that just as a body
has no life without a spirit, so faith without action is dead.

III

Guard Your Speech

[1]   Don't all set yourselves up as teachers, my brothers, but
reflect that those of us who are teachers have to submit to
specially severe criticism. We all make many mistakes, especially
in our conversation. If anyone manages to avoid mistakes in
speech he is completely master of himself, able to exercise
restraint over his whole body. It is like horse-training. When
we put bits into the horses' mouth to make them obey us, we
direct their whole body. Consider the ships too; whatever their
rig and however stiff the breezes that drive them, they are
steered at the will of the helmsman by means of a tiny rudder.
Even so the tongue is a tiny member of the body, yet it makes a
tremendous to-do. What a vast amount of wood is kindled by a
tiny spark! And the tongue is a fire, a universe of iniquity. The

function of the tongue among our members makes it capable of spoiling the whole personality, setting fire to the whole round of existence with a flame kindled in hell. Every kind of beast, bird, insect and fish can be tamed and has been tamed by human beings, but the tongue can no man tame. It is a plague without remedy, full of deadly poison. With it we both praise God our Father and also curse human beings who are made in the image of God. Out of the same mouth flow blessing and cursing. Such things, my brothers, ought not to be. Does a spring pour out fresh and salt water from the same source? Can a fig tree, my brothers, produce olives? Or a vine figs? Of course not. Neither can salt water produce fresh.

Put a Stop to Jealousy—The Quality of Wisdom

[13] Have you any wise and erudite persons among you? Well let them show in the gentleness of their manners the modesty of true scholars. But if any of them cherish bitter jealousy and rivalry in their heart don't let them boast about it. In so doing they are traitors to the truth. Theirs is not the wisdom that comes from above but a worldly wisdom, materialistic, devilish. But where there is jealousy and rivalry, there disorderliness and all sorts of subversive conduct are the rule. But the wisdom that comes from above is first holy, then peaceable, moderate, friendly, full of mercy and kind actions, without any ambiguity or hypocrisy. By such means is a harvest of righteousness prepared in peace by those who work for peace.

IV

The Source of Strife

[1] Where do all your quarrels and antagonisms come from? Does not the cause lie in those passions that are at war in your own personality? You have passionate desires, yet fail to get what you want. You are envious and jealous, yet miss your aim. You fight and quarrel, yet fail to get what you want because you don't ask for it. Or when you do ask, you don't get it because you

ask from a wrong motive, intending to spend God's bounty on your passions. Inconstant creatures! Don't you see that friendship with the world means enmity with God? Whoever chooses to be a friend of the world becomes the enemy of God. Those words were not idly written, 'The human spirit is prone to jealousy'. But God gives us a supply of grace to meet our need. So it is said 'God resists the proud, but gives grace to the humble'. Be submissive then to God. Resist the devil and he will run away from you. Come near to God and He will come near to you. Sinners, mend your ways; clear your minds, you who hesitate. Lament and mourn and weep. Let your laughter be turned to mourning and your joy to sorrow. Humble yourselves before God; and then He will exalt you.

Be Humble with each other and with God

[11] Do not cavil at one another, brethren. He who speaks against his brother or criticizes his brother speaks against the Law or criticizes the Law. Now if you criticize the Law you put yourself in the position not of a law-abiding citizen but a Judge. But there is only one Legislator and Judge—He who has the power of both acquittal and condemnation. Who then are you to criticize your neighbour?

[13] Come now, you who say, 'To-morrow or To-day we will go to a certain city and spend a year there developing our business.' Why, you know nothing about to-morrow. What is your life? It is no more than a wisp of mist, which appears for a moment and then dissolves. So what you ought to say is, 'If it be God's will, we shall live and do this or that.' But you are so proud in your confident boasting. All such pride is wicked, for he who knows what is right and does what is wrong commits sin.

V

Warning to the Rich

Come now, you rich men, weep and howl for the miseries that are coming upon you. Your riches are mouldy, your clothes are moth-eaten, your gold and silver are rusted, and their poison will be a witness against you and will eat into your flesh like fire. Look, the very wages of the labourers who have mown your fields cry out against you because you have not paid on time, and the complaints of your harvesters have reached the ears of the Lord of Hosts. You have been luxurious and dissipated in this world; you have simply nourished yourselves for the day of slaughter. You have condemned and slain the inoffensive man who offered you no resistance.

Comfort for the Rest

[7]   And so, brothers, you must exercise patience in view of the Lord's coming. See how the husbandman waits for his valuable crop, exercising patience until it has been watered by the Spring and Autumn rains. You too must be patient; get a grip on yourselves, for the coming of the Lord is at hand. Refrain from carping at one another, brethren, or you will have judgment passed upon yourselves. Even now the Judge stands at the door. As an example of patient endurance you may take the prophets who spoke in the name of the Lord. Those who held fast we call blessed. You have heard for instance of the patience of Job, and you know how the Lord worked out the climax of that story, showing Himself compassionate and merciful.

[12]   But above all, my brothers, avoid swearing, whether by heaven or by earth or by any other oath. Let a plain Yes or No be sufficient; otherwise you may fall under judgment.

[13]   If any one of you is in trouble, let him pray. If any one of you is enjoying a period of prosperity, let him sing praise. If any one of you is sick, let him summon the elders of the church and let them pray over him and anoint him with oil in the name of the Lord. Believing prayer will save the sick man; the Lord will raise him up; and any sins he has committed will be forgiven him. Therefore confess your sins openly to one another and pray for one another that you may be healed. A good man's prayers have a powerful influence. Elijah was a man of similar passions to ourselves, and he prayed earnestly that it might not rain, and it

did not rain for three years and six months. And he prayed again;
and the sky poured down rain, and the earth produced its crops.

[19] My brothers, if any of you wander from the truth and
someone set him on the right road again, remember that the man
who rescues a sinner from his abandoned ways will save his soul
from death and 'atone for a multitude of sins'.

I Peter

This letter was written to the churches of Asia Minor from Rome (Babylon being a symbolic name for that cruel and Pagan city) at a time when danger of persecution threatened the whole Church. In A.D. 64 the Emperor Nero made Christians the scapegoats for the burning of Rome, and it is probable that S. Peter perished in the subsequent mass executions. But before it was too late he took this opportunity of warning and encouraging the Christians at the other end of the civilized world.

Recognizing the delicacy of their situation he urges them not to give the Pagans any reason to complain of their conduct or to condemn them for any breach of the law, but at the same time, if they are called upon to suffer on the sole ground of being Christians, they should regard that as a most signal honour.

He also bids them compose any differences there may be among themselves and guarantees the genuineness of the teaching given them by Silas (or Silvanus), who was one of their early leaders and was probably both amanuensis and bearer of the letter.

This is sometimes called 'the Epistle of Hope'. It is certainly one of the most gallant and high-hearted letters ever written in circumstances of extreme peril for both author and readers.

I Peter

I

A Letter from Peter, Apostle of Jesus Christ, to the churches of Pontus, Galatia, Cappadocia, Asia and Bithynia.

You are the True Israel, the scattered members of an exiled race, dwelling far from your real Fatherland. Yet through the foreknowledge of God the Father you have been chosen out and set apart for a great destiny. You have been consecrated by the Spirit so as to become obedient to Jesus Christ, and by the sprinkling of His blood you have entered into fellowship with Him, as the old Israel did with Jehovah through the blood of the old Covenant. May He endow you richly with His grace and peace.

The Divine Praises

[3] Blessed be the God and Father of our Lord Jesus Christ, by whose infinite mercy we have been born again to a new life of hope as the result of the resurrection of Jesus Christ from the dead. That is our guarantee that we shall one day receive an inheritance incorruptible, unblemished, imperishable. It is even now being preserved in Heaven for us, who are ourselves preserved by the power of God, through our faith, for a salvation that is waiting to be revealed at the Last Day.

[6] The joy of this expectation is sufficient to make you forget the varied nature of your present trials, which are really intended to assay your faith. When it has been thus tried you will find a genuine residuum, worth far more than gold (for gold perishes in the long run, even though it has been refined in the fire). Then its worth will be recognized with praise and honour and glory at the full revelation of Jesus Christ. Him of course you have not yet seen, but you love Him, and although He is hidden from your eyes, your belief in Him brings you a joy glorious beyond

all expression, because you already anticipate the goal of faith—
the salvation of souls.

[10] Concerning that salvation the old-time prophets made
diligent search and inquiry when they foretold the special favour
that should be yours. They tried to discover to what, or at least
to what sort of, time the Christ-Spirit that was in them pointed,
when it foretold that He would be first a Suffering and then a
Glorified Messiah. To them it was revealed that they were
performing this service not for themselves but for you. And the
good news has now been announced to you by those who first
preached you the Gospel in the power of the Holy Spirit sent
from Heaven.

You should realize how fortunate you are, for even the angels
longed for the chance of seeing this.

Exhortation to Holiness

[13] It follows that you must be continually on the alert, calm
and prepared, with your hopes fixed on the favour that will be
bestowed upon you at the revelation of Jesus Christ. Behave like
obedient children of God, not following the guidance of the old
impulses that moved you in the time of your ignorance. The rule
for you now is that, as the God who has called you is distinguished
from all others by the holiness of His character, so you must try
to be holy in every particular of conduct. Has not He Himself
said, 'Be ye holy as I am holy'? If you appeal to Him as Father
who without any favouritism passes judgment on each man's
work, there must be some element of fear in the way you pass the
time of your earthly pilgrimage.

[18] You know that it was not by perishable means, such as
silver and gold, that you were redeemed from that empty fashion
of life you had inherited from your forebears, but with the
precious blood of Christ, that spotless and unblemished lamb,
who was foreknown before the foundation of the world and has
been made manifest in these last days on your account. By Him
you are encouraged to put your trust in God, who raised Him
from the dead and bestowed upon Him great Glory. So your
faith and hope rest in God.

[22] Again, since you received a spiritual cleansing when you

submitted to the truth and gave evidence of sincerity in affec-
tionate service of the brethren, see that your affection is both
spontaneous and fervent. You are now members not of a mortal
family but of an immortal, brought into existence by command
of the living and eternal God.

> What is man but merely grass
> And all his glory fading flowers?
> Withers the grass: the flowers fall:
> But God's word shall outlast them all.

And that is the word which has been preached to you.

II

Get rid then of each and every taint of malice, deceit, hypocrisy,
envy, slander. As you are still only children in the faith, acquire
a taste for that unadulterated milk which is your natural nourish-
ment, namely Christ, that by means of it you may grow to full
salvation. You have already tasted how good Christ is.

[4] Come then to Him as if He were a live foundation stone—a
stone indeed which has been discarded by human masons but in
the sight of God is the most select and valuable of all. With Him
you yourselves will be built up as living stones into a spiritual
temple, a holy priesthood, for the offering of spiritual sacrifices
acceptable to God through Jesus Christ. So it is recorded in the
Scriptures,

> A new foundation stone, behold, I lay
> Chosen and precious, on Mt. Sion's height.
> Whoso on Him his constant trust shall stay
> Will to the end maintain his honour bright.

[7] That honour belongs to you who are faithful believers. But
for those who are unbelieving 'the stone discarded by the masons'
becomes just a stumbling-block to be tripped over. They stumble
because they are disobedient to God's word. That is the inevitable result of disobedience.

[9] But you are a chosen race, a royal priesthood, a holy nation,
a people for God's own possession; and your special duty is to

proclaim with lips and lives the virtues of Him who has called you out of darkness into His marvellous light. Once you were not a people at all, but now you are the People of God. Once you had no experience of mercy, but now you have experienced mercy in abundance.

Moral Code

[11] Beloved, since you are only temporary sojourners in this world, I call upon you to refrain from worldly passions, which carry on a constant campaign against the soul. Take care that in the sight of the Pagans your conduct is very circumspect, so that, although they now complain that you are rogues, they may be fully aware of the good you do, and may turn to God with thankfulness when the day of trial comes.

[13] To obey the civil authorities is a Christian duty, and you should be careful to perform it, although they may seem to be of merely human appointment. This applies both to the Emperor, as supreme, and also to the provincial governors, who are appointed by him to punish wrong-doing and to reward merit. It is God's will that by your good conduct you should silence foolish and ignorant attacks. You are not slaves but free men, but you must not use your freedom as an excuse for licence: you must use it in a fashion becoming to the slaves of God. So to everyone you should pay their proper respect. To the brethren you should show a special love, to God you should pay reverence, and to the Emperor you should accord loyal honour.

[18] Domestic servants must render obedient and impartial service to their masters—not only to those who are kind and reasonable but also to those who are bad-tempered. You gain favour if in your consciousness of God's continual presence you put up with punishment even when it is wrongfully inflicted. What merit is there in accepting punishment when you have done wrong? But if you are beaten when you have done well, and bear up under it, that wins favour with God. Such indeed is your vocation. For Christ suffered on your behalf, and He has left you a pattern, so that you can follow closely in His footsteps. 'He committed no sin, nor was there any deceit on His lips.' When

people used outrageous words about Him, it was not His habit
to retort in similar terms. He never threatened those who caused
Him pain; rather did He leave His cause to the verdict of the
Just Judge. It was our sins that He bore on His own shoulders to
the cross, in order that we might be set free from sin and live
righteously. 'By His stripes we are healed.' There was a time
when you were like sheep who have strayed from the flock, but
now you have returned to the Shepherd and Bishop of your souls.

III

Married women must render similar obedience to their husbands. In that way a husband who has not accepted the Gospel
may be won over without argument by the behaviour of his wife,
when he has realized the modest respect of her attitude towards
him. Her principal decoration will not be the external adornment of an elaborate coiffure, or trinkets of gold, or a frequently
changed gown, but the hidden virtue of a heart displaying the
fadeless beauty of a friendly and placid disposition, which is a
jewel most precious in the sight of God. That is how the holy
women of old, who fixed their hope on God, adorned themselves
in submission to their husbands. So Sarah obeyed Abraham, and
always called him 'Sir'. You have now become her daughters,
so you must watch your conduct and not allow yourselves to be
disturbed by any commotion in your homes.

[7] Husbands in the same way must apply Christian principles
with intelligence to their relationship with their wives. Just
because the wife is physically the weaker she should be treated
with the more consideration. At least you are equals in your
share of God's good gift of eternal life. If you live in this spirit
there will be nothing to hinder your prayers.

[8] Finally, all of you must have the same disposition, sym-
pathetic, with a brotherly affection for other Christians, charitable
towards all, and humble-minded. You must not try to repay evil
with evil, or cursing with a curse, but on the contrary with kind
words. For you have yourselves been called by God to inherit
nothing but blessing.

The man who wishes life to love
  And days of comfort to enjoy
To speak no wrong it will behove
  And in no guile his tongue employ.

From all ill-will he must depart,
  All good with peace let him ensue.
For God regards the loving heart,
  But evil-doers He'll pursue.

Need for Faithfulness against Persecution

[13] In any case, who will do you any harm if they see you are anxious to do them nothing but good? However, if you do suffer for some good you have done, consider yourselves specially blessed. Don't be afraid of them and don't be disturbed. But in your hearts do homage to Christ as your only Lord, and always be ready to give a reasonable answer to anyone who interrogates you about the hope to which you cling. But give it with gentleness and courtesy, so that although they attack you they may be ashamed when they recognize your good Christian lives. It is better, if we have to suffer at all, to suffer for good deeds than for evil. Christ died once on account of sins, not His own, but the Just for the unjust, in order that He might lead you to God. But it was only in a physical sense that He died: in a spiritual sense He came to life.

[19] In that spiritual condition He went and proclaimed His Good News to the spirits 'in prison', who once had shown marked disobedience in the days when Noah was preparing his ark and the patience of God waited in vain. By entering that ark a few souls, eight in all, were saved. And that was by means of water— a symbol of Baptism, which is our present means of salvation. What we emphasize there is not the washing of dirt from the flesh but our conscientious reply to the question whether we believe in God. That reply we are able to make because of the resurrection of Jesus Christ, who has gone into Heaven and is now on the right hand of God. To Him all angels and all spiritual powers and authorities have been made subject.

IV

Faithfulness against Moral Evil

Fortify yourselves with the thought of Christ's physical sufferings. He who has accepted similar pain for himself has obviously cut himself off from a life of sin. He has shown that he intends to live the rest of his life, not by human passion, but by the will of God. You have already spent quite enough time in living after the Pagan fashion, indulging in unbridled licence, lust, liquor, wine-parties, dissipation, and illegal idolatry. Your boon companions of that time are astonished that you no longer pursue with them the same headlong course of profligacy, and they use harsh words about you. But they will have to render an account to Him who is prepared to judge both the quick and the dead. It was on account of such men that the Gospel was preached to the dead, in order that having received a human judgment during their earthly lives they might now have an opportunity to live a spiritual life by the will of God.

[7] The end of the world is imminent. Don't get excited, but steady yourselves with prayers. Above all practise a fervent love towards one another, for love wipes out another's faults however many they be. Don't grudge any hospitality which you can show to one another. As you have been given resources use them for each other's benefit, like trusted managers who have been given charge of the varied assortment of God's gifts. If a man is a preacher, let him speak with the gravity and authority of one who ministers the revelation of God. If he renders any kind of practical service, let him remember that his power to do it is freely supplied by God. Thus in everything God will be glorified through Jesus Christ, whose is the power and the glory for ever and ever. Amen.

The Present Emergency

[12] Beloved, if you are called upon to face a fiery persecution, don't be amazed as if something extraordinary were happening to you. It is sent to test you; so you should rather rejoice, in pro-

portion as you are called upon to share the sufferings of Christ. Then, when at last His glory is revealed, you will be transported with joy. You are blessed indeed in that you have already had to suffer reproaches on no other ground than that you are Christians, for the Spirit of the glorious Godhead even now rests upon you. But see that none of you has to endure punishment as a murderer, a thief, a rogue, or as a social nuisance busying himself with other men's concerns. On the other hand if anyone suffers as a Christian, let him not be ashamed, but let him give glory to God because that name has been bestowed upon him, and he has an opportunity to endure some hardship for it. The time has come for the Judgment to begin, and in this persecution it is beginning with the Church of God. If it starts with us, how will it end for those who are disobedient to the divine Gospel? If it is only with difficulty that a good man is saved, what will happen to the irreligious and the sinner? So then those who are suffering in accordance with the will of God need only to commit themselves in continued good work into the hands of their faithful Creator.

V

Advice for the Ministry

To those of you who are presbyters I have certain instructions to give, I who am also a presbyter and an eye-witness of the sufferings of Christ and one too who hopes to share with you in the glory that is still to be revealed.

[2] Fulfil your allotted task of tending the flock of God in your neighbourhood, not reluctantly but gladly, as God wishes, not from hope of sordid gain but from devotion, not as tyrants over your cures but as examples to the flock. Then when the Chief Shepherd appears you will receive the reward of a fadeless and glorious crown.

[5] Similarly let the young people be submissive to the presbyters. They should wear humility as their working dress. 'God opposes the proud but gives grace to the humble.'

[6] But first be humble under the mighty hand of God, and then He will exalt you when the right time comes. Hand over

all your anxieties to Him, for you are His care. Don't get excited but be continually on the watch, for the Devil like a roaring lion is continually on the prowl to see of whom he can make a meal. Against him stand steadfast in your faith, remembering that the same tribute of suffering is being paid by the rest of the brotherhood throughout the world. And the God of all grace, who has called you to share His eternal glory in Christ will restore you when your short sufferings are over. He will strengthen you, establish you, give you firm foundations. His is the power for ever and ever. Amen.

Farewell

[12] Silvanus has been my secretary and messenger in the dispatch of this short letter. I wish to record here my conviction that he is worthy of respect and support. My object in writing has been to offer you some encouragement, and I solemnly testify that the doctrine here expressed is what God has revealed. See that you continue faithful in it. The company of God's Chosen, living in this modern Babylon, send their greetings, especially Mark, my son in the faith. Greet one another with the kiss of peace. May all who bear the name of Christ share His tranquillity.

Hebrews

This letter has the same historical background as the last. Persecution has not yet been severe, but at any moment it may be pushed to extremes. The situation of the Christians in Rome was precarious and they would naturally look for means of safety. Since Judaism, as a national cult, was recognized by law, those of them who were Hebrews would be tempted to slip back into their old religion.

The writer, trained in that mixture of Jewish Law and Greek Philosophy which had been developed in the learned circles of Alexandria, finds rich, new arguments in his special studies for their encouragement. He persuades them that Christianity, foreshadowed in the Tabernacle worship of the Old Testament, is the final and absolute religion. He also strengthens their morale by drawing many examples of heroic faith from the past history of their nation.

The letter is anonymous, and efforts to determine who wrote it, however fascinating to scholars, have produced no certain result.

A Letter To Christians
Of Jewish Race

I

Jesus is no mere Angel, but the Son of God

In the old days God spoke to our ancestors in a partial and
inconclusive way through the prophets. Now, at the end of this
era, He has spoken to us through His Son. Him He has made
heir of the whole universe, since it was through His agency that
He created the World. He is the reflection of the Father's Glory
and bears impressed upon Him the very character of the Father.
By the power of His commanding word, the Son sustains the
universe, and now that He has made atonement for sins, He has
sat down on the right hand of the Majesty on high.

The Son's superiority to the angels is revealed to its full extent
in the special Name allotted to Him. To which of the angels has
God ever said, 'Thou art My Son, to-day have I begotten Thee'?
Or again, 'I will be to Him a Father, and He shall be to Me a
Son'? And again, when He brings His beloved Son into the
world He says, 'He shall be worshipped by all God's angels.'
But in regard to the angels, He uses very different language:

'He makes the winds His messengers, His ministers the flaming
fire.'

In one passage the Son is actually addressed as God:

> Thy throne, O God, is set for aye,
>   And justice is Thy sceptre true.
> With Thee the wicked find reward,
>   The righteous gain their promised due.
>
> So Thee for all the feast of life
>   Has God anointed with delight.
> For Thee He sets e'en angels low
>   Since Thou art precious in His sight.

175

> The firm foundations of the World
>   Were laid in time, O Lord, by Thee;
> Thy handiwork the heavens are—
>   Their end in time Thou too wilt see.
>
> Like garments they shall wax full old,
>   The sky a worn-out cloak shall be
> And fall discarded at Thy will,
>   But Thou shalt reign eternally.

What angel did He ever address in language appropriate to a Son? Thus—'Sit Thou on My right hand, till I have subdued Thine enemies and placed them beneath Thy feet.' Then angels are simply spiritual servants sent to minister to those who are to inherit salvation.

II

Jesus makes Men His Brothers

For this reason it is all the more necessary for us to heed carefully the things we are told, lest we drift from our moorings. For if the Law, promulgated by the angels, was strongly enforced, and every slip and act of disobedience visited with just punishment, how shall we escape if we neglect the much greater scheme of salvation offered through the Son? That scheme was announced at the outset by our Lord, and was faithfully transcribed for us by one who actually heard Him. And God Himself has confirmed this testimony by means of signs and wonders and various manifestations of power, distributing gifts of the Holy Spirit as seemed good to Him.

[5] Angels may have the rule in this world, but it was not to them that God subjected the world to come, which is our point of interest at the moment. You can see evidence of this in the verse:

> Is man so great that Thou art to him bound?
>   Does human being merit Thy regard?
> Here less than angels: there with glory crowned:
>   To rule the universe is his reward.

The words 'rule the universe' imply that nothing at all has been left outside the sphere of man's control. Not that we see the whole universe subject to him at the present moment. What we do see is that Jesus, who for a time was put below the rank of angels in order that He might suffer death, has now been crowned with honour and glory so that His participation in death may, by the special favour of God, avail for every man. Thus does Christ lead many 'sons' to glory.

[10] It was fitting, too, that the Pioneer of men's salvation should be made perfect by suffering, and that this should be effected by God Himself, for whom and by whom the whole universe exists. For He who sanctifies and they who are sanctified are all sons of the same Father. That is why He does not disdain to call them brothers: 'I will proclaim Thy Name to my brothers; in the midst of the Church I will sing a hymn to Thee.' Again, 'I will put my trust in Him'; and again, 'Here am I and the children God has given me.'

[14] Since the children share the same flesh and blood, He also shared it with them in order that by dying He might frustrate the one who has control over death (that is, the devil), and set at liberty those who all their life long had been slaves to the fear of death. So when He did become incarnate, it was not the nature of angels that he assumed, but of a certain race of human beings, the descendants of Abraham. It was fitting that He should become in every respect like His brothers in order that He might be a merciful and faithful High Priest in the divine service and effect a proper propitiation for the sins of the people. For since He Himself has been put to the test, He is able to help others who are being tested.

III

The High Priesthood of Christ

So, my good brothers, who all share the same heavenly calling, fix your minds on Jesus, the Apostle and High Priest of our confession. Notice how He shows Himself loyal to Him who appointed Him, just as Moses did in all the duties of God's house.

Jesus has been awarded greater honour than Moses in accordance
with the rule that he who builds and furnishes a house is given
more consideration than the house and household. Every house
is founded by somebody and the founder of the whole universe
is God. Moses was, so to speak, a part of the household, showing
Himself loyal as a servant in all the duties of the House of God.
Thus he bore testimony to the revelation that was still to come.
The loyalty of Christ was quite different: it was like that of a
son in his own home. That Home is made up of ourselves, if we
maintain our boldness and our confident hopefulness to the end.
So the Holy Spirit gives a warning:

> To-day, if His voice you will hear,
>   Do not harden your hearts as of old,
> When your fathers provoked the patience of God,
>   Till their two score years were full told.
>
> With them He was angry and said,
>   'You wander the desert, and err
> In your hearts, not knowing my ways. But I vow
>   That my rest there shall none of you share.'

Take care, my brothers, that none of you become such a traitor
in unbelief as to apostatize from the living God. Strengthen each
other day by day during what remains of 'To-day', so that you
may resist the insidious, hardening effect of sin. We are sharers
with Christ only on condition that we hold fast to the end the
substance of the faith which we received in the beginning. This
will be easier as those lines echo in our ear:

> 'To-day, if His voice you will hear,
>   Do not harden your hearts as of old.'

Who were they who heard His voice and yet made Him angry?
Were they not the whole nation that came out of Egypt with
Moses? And who were they with whom He was vexed forty
years? Were they not the sinners whose corpses fell in the wilder-
ness? And who were they to whom He sware, 'My rest there shall
none of you share'? Were they not those who refused to obey?

It is obvious then that they could not enter into the Promised Land because of lack of faith.

IV

Christ's Promised Rest

The only thing of which we need to be afraid is that, while His promise of future rest still holds good, any of you should seem to come short of His requirements. The good news has come to us just as it came to them. But the message did not benefit them, as it was not received with faith by the hearers. It is only we believers who enter into His rest; as He announced,

> 'With them I was angry and said . . .
>   That My rest there shall none of you share.'

That is in spite of the fact that His course of action was determined from the foundation of the world. This we know from what he says somewhere with regard to a Seventh Day: 'God rested on the Seventh day from all His activities'; which reminds us of the line, 'My rest there shall none of you share.'

[6] Since, however, someone had to enter His rest and the first to receive the good news did not enter because they could not believe it, He fixed another date, 'To-day', repeating after a long interval the old invitation in the Psalms:

> 'To-day, if His voice you will hear,
>   Do not harden your hearts as of old.'

If, however, Joshua had given them rest, He could not have mentioned *another* day. There still remains, therefore, a Sabbath rest for the people of God.

[10] He who enters into that rest drops his activities as God did. Let us then make haste to appropriate it in order not to fall into the old habit of unbelief. The word of God is alive and active with more piercing power than a double-edged sword, penetrating to the very point of division between bone and gristle, between soul and spirit, effecting a critical analysis of the feelings and thoughts of the heart. The result of the analysis is no secret,

but everything is open and exposed to the inspection of Him
with whom we are concerned.

[14] Since, then, we have a great High Priest who has actually
passed through the Heavens, Jesus the Son of God, let us cling
to our profession of faith in Him. Our High Priest is not one who
cannot sympathize with our weaknesses, but One who has been
tested at all points like ourselves and yet has kept free from sin.
Let us then have sufficient boldness to approach the Throne of
Grace; so shall we obtain mercy and find grace to help us in each
and all our necessities.

V

Christ's Universal Priesthood

Every human High Priest is appointed to act on man's behalf
in things Divine so that on the Day of Atonement he may offer
gifts and sacrifices for sins. He is able to bear gently with the
ignorant and the erring because he himself bears all the signs of
human frailty. And that makes it necessary for him to sacrifice
sin-offerings for himself as well as for the people. None of the
High Priests took this honour for himself, but as he was called to
it by God—like Aaron, for example. Nor did Christ usurp the
glory of the Priesthood for Himself, but He was appointed by
Him who said, 'Thou art My Son, this day have I begotten
Thee,' and again, 'Thou art a Priest for ever, of the same type
as Melchizedek.'

[7] Christ, during His life on earth, offered prayers and supplications with urgent crying and tears to Him who could save Him
from death, and He received an answer appropriate to His
devotion. So, although He was God's Son, yet from these experiences He learnt obedience, and when His training was complete, He became the author of eternal salvation to such as gave
obedience to Him; and He was proclaimed by God a High Priest
of the same kind as Melchizedek.

[11] On this point I have much to say which is not easy to
explain, especially since you have become hard of hearing. Just

when, by long standing as Christians, you ought to have become
teachers, you again need someone to explain to you the rudiments
of the most elementary divine truths. You are still such babes
that you need to be fed on milk, not solid food. He who is such
a babe as to require milk is incapable of exercising moral judgment. Solid food is for the grown-ups, for those who through
experience have had their moral sense sufficiently exercised to
distinguish between good and evil.

VI

The Certainty of God's Providence

However, let us leave on one side the rudiments of Christian
doctrine and go on to something more advanced. We will not
bother to lay the foundations all over again, such as repudiation
of the 'dead works' of Jewish legalism; faith in God; the doctrine
of Baptism and Confirmation; the resurrection of the dead and
eternal judgment. God willing, we will take a higher line.

[4] Those who have once seen the light and savoured the
heavenly gift and felt the power of the Holy Spirit and tasted
the good word of God and the energies of the life to come, and
have then apostatized, cannot be restored to repentance, so long
as they thus ostentatiously re-crucify the Son of God. The soil
that drinks in the liberal rain and produces good crops for those
on whose account it is tilled, receives God's blessing, but that
which produces thorns and thistles is good for nothing; it is all
but cursed and will finish in the fire.

[9] But I think a good deal better of you, beloved, though I use
these hard words, and I feel certain that you are on the way to
salvation. God is not so unjust as to forget the loving attention
you have shewn Him in all you have done, and are still doing,
for the Christian brotherhood. I want each one of you to continue to show the same zeal until the end, when hope will be
fulfilled. Don't get slack, but imitate those who already through
faith and endurance have taken possession of the promised
inheritance.

[13]   When God made His promise to Abraham, since there was no one greater than Himself by whom he could take an oath, He swore simply in His own Name, 'Certainly I will give you abundant blessing and will greatly increase your numbers.' Through his constancy, Abraham obtained the fulfilment of that promise. Usually men swear by someone greater than themselves and such an oath puts any doubtful matter beyond dispute. And so God also, in His determination to make clear to the heirs of His promise the unchangeable character of His purpose, interposed with an oath. Thus, by means of two unchangeable things, the promise and the oath, in neither of which it is conceivable that God could lie, sure comfort is given to us who have abandoned everything to lay hold on the hope held out to us. That hope we possess as an anchor of the soul, safe and reliable, fixed in the shrine within the veil, where our precursor Jesus, who has become an eternal High Priest of the type of Melchizedek, has already entered on our behalf.

VII

The King-Priest Melchizedek

This Melchizedek, King of Salem and priest of God Most High, is the one who met Abraham returning from his victorious battle against the Five Kings. We are told that he blessed Abraham and received from him a tenth of the spoil he had taken in the battle. If we translate his name we find it means 'King of Righteousness'; and his title 'King of Salem' means 'King of Peace'. No father is mentioned in connection with him and no mother. In fact, he is without pedigree. Further, no reference is made to his birth or to his death. That is why he is described as belonging to an eternal priesthood. In this he is like the Son of God.

[4]   Consider then what kind of person this was to whom even the patriarch Abraham gave a tenth of his spoil. That action is the more remarkable, because Abraham's own descendants, the Levites, when they entered the priesthood, were given the privelege by law of taking tithes from the people, that is from their

own kith and kin. But here is a man who is not connected with them by race and yet takes tithes of Abraham himself. Not only so, but he actually presumes to give a blessing to one who has already been the recipient of a divine promise. There is no disputing the fact that the proper procedure is for the superior to give the blessing to the inferior. And again, in our case, tithes are received by mortal men, but in this instance, by one of whom it is suggested that he is still alive. We might almost go on to say that to him the Levites, who now receive tithes, then actually paid them through Abraham. For the descendants are naturally included in the ancestor, and Levi was not yet born when his great-grandfather Abraham met Melchizedek.

[11] If perfection could have been reached by means of the Levitical priesthood (for it was around that priesthood that the whole Law was framed), what need could there have been to set up another priest, not of the Aaronic type at all, but of the type of Melchizedek? Obviously a change in the priesthood involves a change in the whole Law under which it serves. He of whom we are speaking belonged to a fresh race of which no member ever served the Altar. Similarly it is clear that our Lord descended from Judah, of which tribe Moses made no mention in connection with the priesthood. So it becomes more evident than ever that there has arrived a new Priest, one of the type of Melchizedek, and that he has been appointed not on the authority of any temporary law, but on the authority of a powerful and indestructible life. That is what is implied in the statement, 'Thou art a priest for ever of the type of Melchizedek.'

[18] The earlier commandment has been set aside because of its weakness and ineffectiveness. The Law was not able to bring anything to perfection. That had to wait for the introduction of a better Hope, which does bring us near to God. The new agreement ushered in by Jesus is better than the old in this respect, that it was affirmed by an oath. The others became priests without any oaths, but Jesus' priesthood was affirmed by an oath—as you can see from what was said to Him, 'Jehovah swore and will not take back his word, "Thou art a priest for ever".' Also, the new priesthood has the advantage in this respect, that the old one has to have many representatives, be-

13

cause death prevents them exercising their office long. Jesus, on the contrary, has no successors in the priesthood, because He lives for ever. That is why He can save to the utmost limit of completeness those who approach God through Him, because He is always alive to make intercession for them.

[26] This was the kind of High Priest that we needed—One who is holy, good, pure, not mixed up with sinners, exalted above the very heavens. He is not under a daily necessity, like other High Priests, to offer sacrifices first for his own sins and then for the people's. One sacrifice only did He offer, and that was when He sacrificed Himself. The Law appoints frail human beings to the High Priesthood, but the statement on oath, which was made after the Law, appoints the Son, in whom is all perfection for evermore.

VIII

The New Agreement

The chief point of all this is that our High Priest is in Heaven, seated on the right hand of the Sovereign Throne, and there he exercises the functions of the sacred ministry in a real Tent of Meeting which was pitched by God and not man. Every High Priest is appointed to offer gifts and sacrifices. It is necessary, therefore, that He, too, should have something to offer. Of course, if the Lord had remained on earth, He would not have been a priest at all, since there are already those who are legally appointed to make all the offerings. But what they minister is only a vague shadow of the celestial reality. That inevitably follows from the instructions given to Moses when he was about to construct the Tent of Meeting. 'Take care,' said God, 'that you make everything in strict accordance with the pattern shown you on the mountain.' Jesus, however, exercises a far higher ministry, just because He was the intermediary of a better agreement between God and man, granted on better terms. It is obvious that the second was necessary only because of defects in the first. These defects were made clear in the indictment pronounced by God against His people.

Behold a time shall come, said God the Lord,
When with the double house of Israel
And Judah an agreement I will make—
But new, not after that old fashion once
I deemed sufficient for your ancestors,
When, grasping firm their faltering hand, I led
Them from captivity in Egypt's waste,
But they ungrateful failed to keep the troth,
And I abandoned them—so saith the Lord.
But now a new agreement I will make
With all the House of Israel, saith the Lord;
Not now on slabs of rock my laws inscribe
But on true hearts that love and understand.
Yea, I will be to them their only God,
And they a loving people be to me.
Nor shall they need henceforth to testify
To brother or to neighbour, 'Know the Lord';
For all shall know me whether small or great.
And mercy will I show them for their sins,
And their transgressions shall be blotted out.

By using the word 'New' He shows that He has suspended the
original agreement. But what has become old and useless is next
door to complete annihilation.

IX

The Tent of Meeting

Now, even the first agreement had its material sanctuary with
its ordered worship. The first portion of the Tent of Meeting was
furnished with lamp and table and shew-bread, and this was
called the Holy Place. And beyond the second curtain was the
tent called the Holy of Holies with its golden Altar of incense and
the ark of the Covenant overlaid with gold, and the golden vessel
containing the Manna, and Aaron's rod that burst into bud, and
the Tables of the Law, and above the ark the cherubim of the
Divine Glory overshadowing the Seat of Mercy. But I cannot
now go into detail about all that.

[6]   When everything had been so arranged the priests regularly entered the first part of the tent to perform their ministrations, but into the second part only one entry was made each year and that by the High Priest alone. His entry had to be marked by the pouring out of blood, which he offered both for himself and for the sins committed in ignorance by the People. Through this ceremonial the Holy Spirit made it clear that so long as the material Tent of Meeting was in existence the way into the spiritual sanctuary could not yet be revealed. That is a kind of parable to illustrate our present condition. The offering of gifts and sacrifices cannot give the worshipper a good conscience : they are merely temporary ordinances, matters of food and drink and various ablutions, arranged until such time as things shall be done properly in the New Order.

[11]   But Christ came as the High Priest of a future perfection, to minister in a Tent of Meeting far vaster and grander than the old, not made by human agency, not belonging at all to this material world. And this He did not by shedding the blood of goats or calves, but at the cost of His own blood. Thus He entered once for all into the Sanctuary and redeemed us for ever. If now those who have incurred defilement can be given ceremonial cleansing through being sprinkled with the blood of goats and bulls, or with the ashes of a heifer, how much more shall the blood of Christ, who through the Eternal Spirit offered Himself an unblemished sacrifice to God, cleanse our conscience from all sham deeds to serve the real and living God.

[15]   For this reason then He became the intermediary of a new agreement, in order that, after the transgressions committed under the first had been expiated by His death, those who had received God's call might enter upon the eternal inheritance which had been promised them. In the case of a testamentary deposition, it is always necessary to prove the death of the testator. A will is valid only on condition of a death, and it is not put into effect as long as the testator is alive. That is why even the first agreement was not inaugurated without blood. When every Commandment had been announced by Moses to the People according to the Law, he took blood of calves and goats with

water and scarlet wool and hyssop, and sprinkled both the document itself and all the people, saying, 'This is the blood of the
agreement that God has concluded with you.' In the same way
he sprinkled the tent and all the sacred vessels with the blood. As
far as the Law is concerned practically everything is made
ceremonially clean by means of blood, and without pouring out
blood there is no absolution from sin.

[23] It was necessary then that the material counterpart of the
heavenly realities should be cleansed by such means, but the
heavenly realities themselves require better sacrifices than these.
Christ did not go into a material sanctuary—a mere copy of the
real one, but into Heaven itself, there to appear before the
presence of God on our behalf. And that He has done, not in
order to make a repeated offering of Himself, like the High Priest
who enters the sanctuary every year (but not with his own
blood!), else He would have had to suffer many times from the
beginning of the world. But now He has appeared once for all
at this culminating point of time in order by the sacrifice of Himself to obtain the remission of sins. It is man's fate to die once for
all and then to face the Judgment. So Christ, now that He has
been offered once for all to remove the sins of the multitude, will
appear a second time to those who waited for His coming. But
this time He will be bearing no sin and will bring salvation.

X

Let us be Faithful to the New Reality

The Law contains only a shadowy suggestion of the New Age,
not the actual reality. That is why, though it offers the same
sacrifices every year in perpetuity, it cannot guarantee perfection
for those who bring them. Otherwise, would they not have
stopped bringing them, if the worshippers had been made clean
and no one of them any longer suffered from an evil conscience?
But as it is, there is a reminder of sins every year for the simple
reason that you cannot do away with sin just by using the blood
of bulls and goats. That is why, when Christ came down to earth,
He said:

No other sacrifice desiredst Thou
　　Than that same body which Thou gavest me,
And so I said, 'I pay my lawful vow:
　　Thy gift's accepted and returned to Thee.'

You notice He first says, 'No other sacrifice desiredst Thou' (that means, of course, that God rejects the sacrifices offered under the Mosaic Law), and then He goes on to say, 'Thy gift's accepted and returned to Thee.' Thus He supersedes the first agreement in order to establish a new one. As a result of His determination to do this our sanctification has been brought about through the one unique offering of the Body ('accepted and returned') of Jesus Christ.

[11]　Every priest stands daily ministering in the Temple and offering the same sacrifices many times over, although they are utterly powerless to take away sins. But Christ offered once for all a perpetual sacrifice for sin and then took His seat at God's right hand, hence-forward waiting for the time when all His enemies should be made subject to Him. By that one offering He made perfect for ever those who were being sanctified.

[15]　Testimony is borne to the truth of this statement by the Holy Spirit Himself. For after saying—

This is the covenant I'll make with them,
　　When all those days are ended, saith the Lord;
My laws will I inscribe within their hearts,
　　And on their minds will write them evermore,

He then goes on to say—
'No more their guilt and sin will I recall.' But when remission of sins has been granted, there is no longer any need of a sin offering.

[19]　Since then, my brethren, in virtue of the blood of Christ we can be so bold as to enter the Sanctuary by that sacred and living road which He has opened up for us through the veil of His flesh, and since we have a great priest over the House of God, let us draw near with a true heart and assured faith after ablutions which have not only cleansed our bodies with pure water,

but have freed our hearts from consciousness of guilt. Let us cling to the statement of our hope without any weakening, for He who gave us the promise is utterly trustworthy. And let us stir each other up to mutual emulation in love and kind deeds, not playing truant from our Church meetings (as some do), but giving each other that mutual encouragement which becomes all the more necessary as we see the Last Day drawing near.

[26] If we sin deliberately after having been told the truth, there is no fresh sacrifice for us to offer. All that is left for us is a sort of fearful expectation of judgment and of fiery Wrath, which will devour all opponents. Anyone who disobeys a Law of Moses dies without mercy on the evidence of two or three witnesses. Of how much severer punishment will he be deemed worthy who has trodden under foot the Son of God, despised the Blood of the Agreement by which he was sanctified, and insulted the Spirit of Grace. We know who said, 'Vengeance is mine, I will repay,' and again, 'The Lord will judge His people.' We may well be afraid of falling under the censure of the Living God.

[32] Recall the early days when you were first converted and how you were then tested by having to endure much suffering. That occurred both when you yourselves were made to appear ridiculous by having insults and injuries heaped upon you and also when you associated with others who were being so treated. You showed practical sympathy with those who were imprisoned, and you submitted gladly to the confiscation of your goods, knowing that you had better and abiding possessions. Don't lose that confidence; some day it will be well rewarded. Perseverance is necessary so that you may do the will of God and receive the fulfilment of His promise:

> A very little time doth still betide,
>   And He who comes shall come and not be slow,
> The just man now in simple faith must bide,
>   In naught he'll please me if he shrink from woe.

But we are not of those who 'shrink' and come to ruin, but of those who show faith and win salvation.

XI

Faith

Now faith is a conviction of the fulfilment of our hopes, and a continual reliance upon the unseen world. By it the Patriarchs were enabled to make their witness to the supernatural. It is faith that reveals how the worlds were created by the Word of God, so that what is seen owes its origin to what is not seen. It was by faith that Abel offered to God a better sacrifice than Cain and so proved his own righteousness, God adding His testimony by accepting his gifts. Thus, though he is dead, Abel still speaks by his faith. As a result of faith, Enoch was carried up from the earth and never experienced death. 'He was never found, for God carried him away.' But before he was carried away, testimony was borne to him that he pleased God. Without faith it is impossible to please Him, for every one who approaches Him must believe first that He exists and then that He will receive those who seek Him.

[7] It was by faith that Noah was warned of things as yet invisible, and out of his reverence for God prepared an Ark for the safety of his household; by so doing he passed judgment on the society of his day and became the rightful inheritor of the righteousness that springs from faith. It was by faith that Abraham obeyed the call to go to the place that he was to receive as his patrimony, and set out on his journey without knowing where he was going. By faith he settled in the Land of Promise, although it was a foreign country, living in tents with Isaac and Jacob, who shared with him the same expectations. He looked forward to that permanent city whose architect and builder is God. It was by faith that Sarah received power to conceive long after her climacteric was passed, for she considered Him reliable who gave her the promise; and so from one who was as good as dead there sprang a nation like the stars of heaven in multitude and as innumerable as the grains of sand on the sea shore.

[13] These all died in faith without having actually received the things promised—they only saw them from a distance, but they hailed the sight with joy, acknowledging that, as far as this

world was concerned, they were no more than strangers and
exiles. People who make that kind of acknowledgment show that
they are on the look-out for a true fatherland. If they thought
much of the land from which they came, they would no doubt
find occasion to return; but as it is they long for a better country,
that is to say a territory in Heaven. For this reason God con-
descends to be known as their God, and He has made them His
people by preparing a city for them.

[17]   It was by faith that Abraham, when he was put to the test,
showed himself ready to sacrifice Isaac. He who had received
the promises offered his only son, although he had been told,
'From Isaac shall your descendants come.' He argued that God
could raise them even from the dead. And by a sort of acted
parable he did receive Isaac from the dead.

[20]   By faith, too, Isaac conferred a blessing of future greatness
on Jacob and Esau. By faith, Jacob, when he was at the point of
death, blessed each of the sons of Joseph, and stood up to worship,
supporting himself by his staff. By faith Joseph at the end of his
life foretold the Exodus of the Israelite people from Egypt and
gave directions concerning the disposal of his bones. By faith
Moses at his birth was hidden by his parents for three months,
because they saw he was a fine child, and they dared to disobey
the King's command. By faith Moses when he was grown up,
refused to be called the son of Pharaoh's daughter, preferring to
suffer misfortune with God's people rather than to enjoy the
fleeting pleasures of sin. He reckoned a share in the reproaches
poured upon the Messiah as greater riches than all the treasures
of Egypt, for he had an eye to the final reward. It was by faith
that he fled from Egypt and not for fear of the King's anger. He
displayed the enduring courage of one who fixes his gaze on the
Invisible King. By faith he kept the Passover and sprinkled the
houses with blood so that the Destroying Angel should not touch
the Israelites' firstborn. It was faith that enabled him to cross the
Red Sea as if he was walking on dry land, while the Egyptians
making the same attempt were drowned.

[30]   It was faith that caused the walls of Jericho to fall down
after the Israelites had marched round them for seven days. It

was faith that saved the prostitute Rahab from perishing with the infidels; for she had received the spies peaceably.

[32] But why should I continue the list? I have no time to speak of Gideon, Barak, Samson, Jephthah, David, Samuel and the prophets. By faith they conquered Kingdoms, established justice, obtained the fulfilment of promises, were delivered from the mouths of lions, quenched the heat of a furnace, escaped death by the sword, received strength in place of weakness, became heroes in battle, and put to flight hosts of enemies. Women welcomed their dead back from the other world. Others put aside all hopes of deliverance and were broken on the wheel, that they might be raised again to a better life. Some were tested by being mocked and flogged or by being actually chained and imprisoned. They were stoned, they were put to the ordeal, they were quartered, they were beheaded. Others were outcast, their only clothing the skin of a sheep or a goat; they were destitute, afflicted, ill-treated, although they were altogether too good for this world. They fled to the deserts and the mountains and lived in caves and gullies.

[39] But even they, although they were all proved by their trials to possess faith, did not receive the promised reward. God delayed the fulfilment of His promise out of His beneficent purpose to us: they had to wait for us in order that we might all be perfected together.

XII

Face your Difficulties

Now this great host of heroes fills the spectators' seats around the arena in which our contest is to take place. To do well in their eyes we must get rid of every ounce of superfluous weight and of every hampering sin, and we must run with endurance the course that is set for us. But we must keep our eyes fixed on our goal, which is none other than Jesus Himself, the founder and perfecter of our faith. He for a future joy endured the pain and scorned the disgrace of crucifixion, and in the end took His place at the right hand of God. You should indeed take a pattern from

Him, who puts up with such hostility on the part of sinful men. It will prevent you from growing tired and being deflected from your purpose. You have not yet been called upon to shed your blood in conflict with sin. And you have forgotten that comforting passage in which you are appealed to as sons:

> Despise not, son, the chastening of the Lord,
>   Nor, when rebuked, in chagrin miss your aim,
> For in correction is His love revealed,
>   And the son punished is the son received.

You should put up with such correction, for then is God treating you as sons.

[7] Is there any father who does not correct his own child? If you are spared the correction with which everyone else has to put up, then you are not sons but bastards. When our earthly fathers correct us we render them respect: much more then ought we to obey our Heavenly Father, and so make sure of Eternal Life. They exercise a temporary correction at their own caprice, but He does it for our good that we may be made sharers in His Holiness.

[11] No correction seems at the moment to be pleasant, but distinctly unpleasant. Afterwards, however, those who are subjected to it gain as a result both peace and righteousness. So, 'Lift up your inert hands and straighten your sagging knees, and set a straight course for yourselves. Then the lame will not be tripped up, but will have a chance of being healed.'

[14] Try to live at peace with everyone, and aim at attaining that holiness without which no one shall see God. Exercise such vigilance that none may miss the grace of God, and that no corruption take root among you to poison your relations with one another, and that there be among you no immoral person or frivolous man like Esau, who surrendered his birthright for a single plate of food. You know that afterwards when he wished to obtain the blessing due to him as firstborn, he was rejected; for he found no opportunity of undoing the past, though he sought it with tears.

[18]   You are not supplicants at Mt. Sinai with its material fire already aflame, with its cloud and smoke and wind, its echoing trumpet and thundering words. These last were so awe-inspiring that they who heard them asked that no more should be said. The instruction, 'If even a beast touch the mountain, it shall be stoned', was too much for them. Indeed, so awe-inspiring was the scene that Moses himself said, 'I am trembling with fright.'

[22]   But you have come to Mt. Sion and to the City of the Living God, the Heavenly Jerusalem, and to the assembly of a myriad angels, and to the Church and congregation of God's beloved sons whose names are enrolled in Heaven, and to God Himself who is Judge of all, and to the spirits of the good who have now been made perfect, and also to Jesus who is the intermediary of the New Agreement, and to His sprinkled blood which makes a far finer appeal than did that of Abel when it cried from the ground for vengeance.

[25]   Be careful that you don't neglect that appeal. If they did not escape who ignored the blood crying from the ground, we shall certainly not escape if we turn deaf ears to the voice that appeals from Heaven. That voice once convulsed the earth, but now it has given an assurance, 'The next and last time I will convulse not only the earth but also Heaven'. That phrase, 'The next and last time', suggests the annihilation of the things convulsed, because they are created, material things; but it involves as a consequence the continuance of all the things that do not suffer from the convulsion. Since then you and I possess an unshakeable Kingdom, let us show such grace as to serve God acceptably with piety and reverence. For the God who consumes by fire is our God, too.

XIII

Practical Service

Be careful then to maintain your close friendship with one another within the circle of the Christian Church. And don't neglect the claims of hospitality. By showing themselves hospitable to strangers some have entertained angels unawares. Keep

in mind those who are in prison as vividly as if you were imprisoned with them. Remember, too, those who are suffering
persecution, realizing that as long as you live you also are liable
to suffer.

[4] Let the holy estate of matrimony be held in universal
esteem, and let no one break its laws. Fornicators and adulterers
fall under the judgment of God. Let your way of life be free
from all love of money, and be satisfied with such possessions as
you have. For has not God Himself said, 'I will not leave you
or forsake you'? And that encourages us to reply, 'Since the
Lord is my helper, I will not be afraid: what power has any
human being to do us harm'?

[7] Guard the memory of your leaders who have taught you
the word of God. Remember how they met their end and imitate
their faith. Jesus Christ is for you just what He was for them,
the same yesterday, to-day and for ever. Don't go astray after
all sorts of weird doctrines. If you need courage, see that it is
kept up by grace, not by reliance on any particular kind of food,
whether sacrificial or other. That has never been of any use,
even to those who took infinite pains over it. We Christians have
our own Altar at which they have no right to eat who share in the
ministries of the Tent of Meeting. There the blood of certain
beasts was offered for sin by the High Priest in the sanctuary, and
then their carcases were burnt outside the camp. Similarly
Jesus, in order that He might sanctify His people by His own
blood, suffered outside the gate. And so let us go out and join
Him outside the Camp, even if it does mean that we must bear
the same reproach.

[14] In this world we have no permanent abode, but we are on
the look-out for the city that is still to come. Through Jesus, then
let us continually offer our thank-offering to God, that is the
fruit of lips that acknowledge allegiance to Him. And don't
forget good works and all the duty of sharing with others, for
that is the kind of sacrifice that pleases God. Trust your leaders
and obey them, for they watch over your souls knowing that
they must one day render their account. Make it possible for

them to do so with joy and not with grief; for what brings grief to them could be of no value to you.

[18]   Pray for me. I don't mean to suggest by that request that I have any doubts about my conscience being clear or about my efforts in every respect to lead a good life. But I am especially anxious for you to pray that I may be able to return to you soon. May the God of Peace, who, after the Lord Jesus had shed His blood to confirm the Eternal Agreement, restored from the dead that great Shepherd of the sheep, establish you in every kind of goodness so that you may do His will and that we may all be made a source of satisfaction to Him by means of Jesus Christ, whose is the glory for ever and ever, Amen.

[22]   I beg you, brothers, to take in good part the advice I have given you. I apologize for the shortness of this letter. You have no doubt heard that Brother Timothy has been set free. If he arrives soon, I will bring him with me to pay you a visit.

[24]   Give my greetings to all your leaders and to all the other members. The Italians send their kind regards. Grace be with you all.

Jude

Like the Epistle of *James*, this letter was probably written by a 'brother' of our Lord, thus giving further evidence of the importance of His family in the Church. Both letters have about them a strongly Jewish atmosphere, but the present writing is specially interesting for its use of apocryphal and frequently of apocalyptic books, such as were produced during the period between the close of our Old Testament and the opening of the New. Thus in v. 9 there is a reference to the Assumption of Moses, and in v. 14 to the Book of Enoch.

The author had intended to write a general letter on Christian doctrine, but the sudden appearance of a specially vicious type of false teaching imposed upon him a more definite aim and subject. A set of malcontents had arisen who claimed that because they possessed the Spirit they were therefore free both from the authority of the official leaders and also from the restraints of the moral law. The measure of the danger inherent in such teaching can be judged from the vehemence with which *Jude* refutes it.

The Letter Of Jude

A letter from Jude, slave of Jesus Christ and brother of James, to the Chosen, who are beloved in God the Father and preserved in Jesus Christ. Mercy, peace and love be yours in abundance.

Purpose

[3] Beloved, I was busy writing to you on the subject of our common salvation, when the necessity suddenly arose to write and urge you to throw yourselves into a new contest on behalf of that faith which was handed over once for all to the keeping of the Christian folk. Certain men have stealthily insinuated themselves into your congregation, ungodly men, who on this account have been foredoomed of old to punishment. They have turned God's gracious gift of freedom into an opportunity for licence, and they have betrayed our only Lord and Master, Jesus Christ.

Warning

[5] I want to remind you, since you have already been told it all before, that when Jehovah saved the People out of Egypt He afterwards destroyed those who refused to believe. Also the angels who relinquished the care of their own domain and deserted their proper abode He has committed to darkness, to be kept in everlasting bonds until the Judgment of the Great Day. Sodom and Gomorrha with the neighbouring cities, which in the same way practised immorality and gave themselves up to unnatural lusts, provide us with a third example; for they suffer the punishment of eternal fire.

The False Teachers

[8] In just the same way these dreamers of pretended visions are contemptuous of all constituted authority, whether natural or supernatural, and rail against angelic dignities. But even the Archangel Michael, when he was preparing to bury the body of

Moses, and Satan laid claim to it, was not moved by the heat of argument to make any railing accusation against his opponent, but merely said, 'The Lord rebuke thee, Satan.' These men, however, hide their ignorance under the loudness of their charges, and such instinctive knowledge as they share with the brute creation they use merely as an opportunity of eternal self-destruction. They are doomed; they tread the way of Cain and fling themselves headlong into the error of Balaam, who sold his prophecies for payment; they will be destroyed in their rebellion, as Korah was in his.

Their Use of the Agape

[12] These men are blots on your love-feasts, when they have the audacity to feed with you. They certainly get good fodder out of it for themselves. They are clouds that give no rain, driving all ways before the wind. They are like trees in autumn that bear no fruit, doubly dead, torn up by the roots. Like the raging waves of the sea they cast up nothing but refuse. They are like shooting stars, for which is reserved utter and final darkness for ever.

Enoch's Prophecy

[14] It was of these that Enoch prophesied, although he lived so long ago as to be only six generations removed from Adam. He said, 'Behold the Lord cometh with the myriads of His holy ones to pass sentence upon all, and to convict all the ungodly of all the ungodly deeds that they have committed in such ungodly fashion and of all hard things that ungodly sinners have spoken against Him.' These are the people who grumble and grouse against authority and pursue their own passions. Their conversation is full of bombastic boasting, but at the same time they are ready to use fulsome flattery to anyone of whom there is a chance to make gain.

Exhortation to be Faithful

[17] But you, beloved, remember what you were told before by the Apostles of our Lord Jesus Christ. They used to say, 'In the last times there will be libertines who will scoff at your self-

14

restraint while they follow the guidance of their ungodly passions.'
Such men are factious, sensual, devoid of Spirit. But you,
beloved, build yourselves up on the foundations of your most
holy faith, and pray in the power of the Holy Spirit, keeping
yourselves in the sphere of God's love and looking forward to the
revelation of the mercy of our Lord Jesus Christ, which will lead
you into life eternal. When you are called upon to pass judgement on others, treat them with discrimination. Meet the arguments of the disputatious; rescue others like logs plucked from
the fire; still others you must hold at arm's length, hating to
touch even the clothes they wear, which share in the defilement
of their guilt. Such, if necessary, you must excommunicate.

Doxology

[24] Now to Him who is able to keep you from stumbling and
to present you spotless and exultant before His glory, to our only
God and Saviour through Jesus Christ our Lord be glory,
majesty, might and power, as it was in the beginning, is now
and ever shall be. Amen.

I, II, and III John

These three letters were all written by the author of the Fourth Gospel and were probably addressed from the same town, Ephesus. The first is an encyclical; the second is inscribed to 'The Elect Lady', who may be a church rather than a particular individual; the third is addressed to a certain Gaius of whom no knowledge has come down to us.

The purpose of the first two letters is the same as that of the Fourth Gospel, namely, to show that although Jesus Christ is certainly the incarnation of the eternal Word or Thought of God, yet He was no mere phantasmal appearance, as some had begun to teach, but an actual flesh-and-blood reality. In other words, He was really man as well as really God.

The third letter deals with a particular problem of early Christian organization, that of hospitality for the travelling agents of the Church. Such entertainment was regularly and freely given. But that very fact opened the door to many impostors and false teachers. John urges Gaius to see that duly authorized persons receive official hospitality.

S. John's First Letter

I

The Word of Life

I am going to write to you about the Word of Life. He existed from the beginning, before time was; yet I have listened to Him; I have seen Him with my own eyes; I have really looked at Him, and have touched Him with my own hands. What that Word revealed to us was Life. I have really seen Eternal Life. And now I am testifying to it and announcing it to you. That Life was with the Father, and yet it was revealed to us. I am telling you about something that I have actually seen and heard, in order that you, too, may share our comradeship in this knowledge. And that comradeship of ours is with the Father and with His Son, Jesus Christ. The reason why I am writing to you on this subject is that I want your joy to be complete.

The Nature of God

[5] This is the message that I heard from Him and now hand on to you, that 'God is light and in Him is no darkness at all'. If we say that we are in partnership with Him and yet choose to live in darkness, we are telling an untruth and not being sincere. But if we choose to live in the light, as He is in the light, we share a real partnership, and the blood of Jesus, His Son, washes us clean from every sin. If we say that we are without sin, we are self-deceived and there is no truth in us. But if on the contrary we openly confess our sins, He is so just and reliable that He will not only forgive us our sins, but will wash us clean from all unrighteousness. If we affirm that we have never sinned, we make Him a liar and His truth is not in us.

II

Sin and its Remedy

My children, I am writing to help you to keep clear of sin. If anyone does sin, we have One who will plead our cause with the

Father, Jesus Christ the righteous. He has made Himself the
propitiatory offering for our sins, and not for ours only, but for
those of the whole world.

[3]   But, you may ask, how can we know that we have a saving
knowledge of Him? By the fact that we keep His commandments. If anyone says that he has such a knowledge and yet fails
to keep His commandments, he is obviously a stranger to the
truth. But when a man succeeds in keeping God's word, then
indeed the Divine love has come to perfection in him. Here is
the test by which we may know that we are one with Him: the
man who says he abides in Christ ought to conduct himself
precisely as Christ did.

Obedience in Love and Light

[7]   Beloved, it is no new commandment that I lay upon you,
but an old commandment which has been laid upon you from
the beginning. It is an old commandment because it has always
formed the subject of the teaching you have received. On the
other hand, it is a new commandment in the sense that it was
first fully made clear in Christ and then in yourselves; for the
darkness is only now passing away and the light is just beginning
to shine. The man who says he is in the light and nourishes
hatred against his brother is really in the darkness even now.
On the other hand, the man who loves his brother keeps himself
in the light and no one can stumble over him. He who hates his
brother is in darkness, he walks in darkness and cannot tell where
he is going because the darkness blinds him.

An Appeal

[12]   Children, I write to you because your sins have been forgiven through His name.
       Fathers, I write to you because you have known Him who
has existed from the beginning.
    Young men, I write to you because you have overcome the
Evil One.
    Yes, I have written to you, children, because you have known
the Father.

I have written to you, fathers, because you have known Him who has existed from the beginning.

I have written to you, young men, because you are strong, and the word of God has established itself in you, and you have overcome the Evil One.

[15] This is what I want to say, Don't give yourselves to the service of this world or to anything that belongs to this world. Love of this world excludes all desire to serve the Father. Everything that belongs to this world, the passion of the flesh, the desire of the eyes, the vainglory of life, proceeds not from the Father, but from the world. The world and its desires pass away, but he who does the will of God stands fast for ever.

Conflict of Truth and Falsehood

[18] Children, the last hour has come. You have heard that it is to be marked by the advent of the antichrist. Well, there are now many antichrists; so we know that it is the last hour. They used to be members of the Church, but they never really belonged to us. If they had truly belonged to us, they would have remained with us. But they left us and so made it clear that not one of them really belonged to us.

[20] You, of course, in virtue of your anointing by the Holy Spirit, have all acquired Christian knowledge. I have not written to you because you don't know the truth, but because you do know it and therefore realize that nothing false can belong to the truth.

[22] There is no falsehood so great as the denial of the Messiahship of Jesus. The man who denies that is the real Antichrist, because with that falsehood he denies both the Father and the Son. No one can deny the Son without denying the Father also.

[24] See to it that you keep firm hold of the truth you were taught in the beginning. If you do so, you will keep your hold of both the Father and the Son. And to do that is to realize the promise that He Himself gave you, namely, Eternal Life.

[26] I am writing this to warn you against those who would lead you astray. But as far as you are concerned the anointing

you have received from Him remains with you, and you have no
need of anyone to teach you. The anointing with His Spirit,
which you received from Him, gives you instruction on every
point, and it is truth and not falsehood. Remain then firm in
fellowship with Him as His Spirit has taught you.

[28] And so, my children, abide in Him, that when He comes
again you may have plenty of confidence and not be put out of
countenance at His appearing. If you know that He is good,
you know that everyone who practices goodness is His son.

III

Children of God

How great is the love the Father has shown us in thus allowing
us to be called the children of God. And such indeed we are.
This is the reason why the world will not recognize us, because
it would not recognize Him. Beloved, we actually are the children of God now. What we shall be in the future has not yet been
made clear. We know that when He appears we shall be like
Him, because we shall see Him as He is. Everyone who rests
such a hope on God tries to make himself holy as God is holy.

[4] Everyone who commits sin is guilty of lawlessness, for sin is
lawlessness. You know that He appeared to take away sins, and
in Him is no sin. Everyone who remains in Him abstains from
sin. Everyone who continues in sin has failed either to recognize
or to know Him. Children, don't let anyone deceive you. He
who does righteous deeds is righteous, even as He is righteous.
He who continues in sin is of the Devil, for the Devil has been
a sinner from the beginning. That is the reason why the Son of
God appeared, that He might neutralize what the Devil had
done.

[9] Everyone who is a son of God abstains from committing sin,
because he inherits his Father's character. He cannot live a life
of sin because he is a child of God. That is how you can tell the
difference between God's children and the Devil's: anyone who
does not act righteously and does not love his brother is not of

God. This is the message you heard at the outset, that we love one another. We are not like Cain, who was of the Evil One and killed his brother. And why did he kill him? Because his deeds were wicked and his brother's righteous.

Brotherhood in Christ

[13] Don't be surprised, brothers, if the world hates you. We know that we have changed over from death to life because we love our brothers. The person who has no such love remains in a condition of death. Anyone who hates his brother is a murderer, and we know that no murderer can possess Eternal Life. We understand the nature of love from the fact that Christ laid down His Life on our behalf. Similarly we ought to lay down our lives for the brethren. If the man who has plenty of this world's goods sees his brother in need and withholds compassion from him, how can there be any love of God in him? Dear children, don't let us be satisfied with a love shown only in words, but let us translate it into sincere deeds. By this means we shall recognize that we are on the side of truth and shall satisfy any scruple of conscience we may feel in His presence. If we feel any such scruples, we shall remember that God is superior even to our conscience and knows all about us.

[21] Beloved, if our conscience is clear, then we can approach God boldly, and whatever we ask He will give it us because we keep His commandments and do the things of which he approves. This is His commandment, that we believe in the person of His Son, Jesus Christ, and continue to love one another according to Christ's instructions. He who keeps God's commandments lives in God and God in him. How we know that we live in Him is that we possess His Spirit, which He gave us when we became Christians.

IV

Rivalry between Truth and Error

Beloved, you must not trust every impulse that claims to be spiritual, but you must test every such influence to see whether it really comes from God. Many false prophets have emerged in our modern world. This is how you can distinguish the Spirit of God: every ecstatic utterance that proclaims Jesus to be the Messiah in actual flesh and blood is of God, and every such utterance that denies the statement is not of God. This latter is the spirit of Antichrist, about whose coming you have heard. It is now already here in the world. But you, children, are of God, and have risen superior to the false prophets, because He who is in you is greater than he who is in the world. They are of the world and so they talk of worldly things, and the world listens to them. We are of God; he who knows God listens to us. But he who is not of God does not listen to us. That is how we distinguish between the spirit of truth and the spirit of error.

God and Love

[7] Beloved, let us love one another, for love is of God, and everyone who loves is born of God and knows God. He who does not love can never have known God, for God is love. The love of God has been made clear to us in this fact, that God sent His only Son into the world that through Him we might live. Love, I say, is shown in this fact—not that we loved God, but that He loved us and sent His Son as an atonement for our sins. Beloved, if God loved us so much as that, we ought to love one another. No one has ever seen God, but if we love one another He dwells in us and it is His love that is brought to completion in us.

[13] This is how we know that we dwell in Him and He in us, because He has given us a share of His Spirit. And I have actually seen, and bear witness to the fact, that the Father has sent His Son as Saviour of the world. Whoever confesses that Jesus is the Son of God, God dwells in him and he in God. And we know and have believed the love that God feels for us.

The Activity of Love

[16] God is love, and he who lives in a condition of love lives in God, and God lives in him. Love does not complete its work with us until it has given us confidence to meet the judgment of the Last Day. Such confidence arises out of the assimilation of

our character to that of Christ in this life. In love there is no such
thing as fear; complete love excludes fear, for fear arises from
dread of punishment. Anyone who feels such dread has not
completely learnt love (and so lacks confidence).

[19] We practise love because He first loved us. If anyone says,
'I love God' and hates his brother, he is untruthful. The man
that does not love his brother, who is before his very eyes, cannot
love God, whom he has never seen at all. Besides, it is God's
own commandment to us that anyone who loves God must love
his brother also.

V

Power of the Christian Life

Everyone who believes that Jesus is the Messiah is a son of God,
and he who loves the Father must love the children. So we know
that we love the children of God, if we love God and keep His
commandments. For that is what the love of God is—the keeping of His commandments. And those commandments are not
burdensome, as is proved by the fact that all God's children
conquer the world. The means by which we conquer the world
is our faith. Is there any other world-conqueror than the man
who believes that Jesus is the Son of God? Jesus Christ—He it is
who came into the world, not as a mere phantom, but with a true
physical body, composed, like that of every human being, of
water and blood. And the Spirit bore testimony to this real
incarnation, because the Spirit is truth.

[8] There are thus three evidences in support of Jesus—the
Spirit, the water, and the blood; and these three are really one.
If we are willing to receive human testimony, we should realize
that divine testimony is even better. And that is the testimony
actually given by God on behalf of His Son, for he who believes
on the Son of God has the testimony in himself. Any man who
does not believe God has made Him a liar, because he has not
accepted the testimony that God has given concerning His Son.
This is the testimony, that God gave us eternal life and that life

is in His Son. He who possesses the Son possesses life, and he who
does not possess the Son does not possess life.

Epilogue . . . Confidence

[13]   I have written to you in this strain in order to assure you
that you are in possession of eternal life—you who believe in the
revealed Person of the Son of God. I have such confidence with
regard to Him as to be assured that if we ask anything in accordance with His will He will listen to us. And if we know that He
will listen to us whatever we ask, we know that we shall obtain
the favours we ask of Him.

[16]   If for instance a man sees his brother committing some not
very grievous sin, he can ask and God will grant him life for those
who do not sin very grievously. There is a kind of sin that is fatal.
I do not suggest that he should pray for that. All wrong-doing is
sin, but there is a kind of sin that is not fatal.

[18]   We know that everyone who is born of God abstains from
sin: the Son of God preserves him and the Evil One cannot get
hold of him. We know also that, whereas the world is under the
influence of the Evil One, we belong to God. We know, too, that
the Son of God has come and has given us understanding to
recognize the true God. That is how we come to be so closely
united to that true God, because we are already one with His
Son, Jesus Christ, and Jesus Christ is Himself both true God and
Eternal Life.

My sons, avoid all idolatrous imitations.

S. John's Second Letter

From the Elder to the chosen lady and her children.

Greetings

[1] I send you my love, for I do love you all truly, and not only I but all who know the truth. We must do so because we are united in the possession of the truth, which will remain with us for ever. Grace, mercy and peace shall be ours, as a gift from God the Father and from Jesus Christ, His Son, in truth and love.

I was very glad to find some of your children walking in the way of truth, as our Father has instructed us.

Purpose

[5] And now, dear lady, I have a request to make of you—not that I wish to lay any new commandment on you, but just the old one which we have had from the beginning, namely, that we love one another. This is what love means, that we walk in the way of God's commandments. That is His commandment as it was given us from the beginning, in order that we should rule our conduct by it.

[7] But it happens that there are many false teachers abroad in the world who do not acknowledge that Jesus Christ has come in the flesh. Such a teacher is an impostor and an antichrist. Look after yourselves, so that you do not lose what we have been working for, but gain a full reward. Anyone who is too 'progressive' to abide by the teaching of Christ is cut off from God, but he who abides by Christ's teaching is in union with both the Father and the Son.

A Request

[10] If anyone comes to you and does not bring this teaching. don't receive him into your house, and don't give him a welcome, Anyone who welcomes him shares in his evil deeds.

[12] I have a lot to tell you, but I would rather not do it on paper. However, I hope to come and tell you by word of mouth. This is joyful news for us both.

Your sister's children (she is another of God's chosen) send you their greetings.

S. John's Third Letter

From the Elder to my dear Gaius, who is my friend in the comradeship of the truth.

Greetings

[1] Dear friend, my prayer for you is that in all things you may prosper and keep in health, as I know you already prosper in spiritual matters. I was very glad when from time to time some of the brothers came and brought me news of the sincerity of your life and told me how consistently you walk in the way of truth. I have indeed no greater pleasure than to hear that my children in the faith live consistent Christian lives.

Hospitality

[5] My friend, it is a loyal act on your part to render service to members of our faith, especially to such as are strangers. Many of them have reported on your kindness in our church meeting. You will be doing well to forward on their journey in a manner befitting our religion the men of a similar type who are the bearers of this letter. They have set out on a mission for the Name of God, and they have refused any help from Pagans. It is therefore our duty to offer them hospitality, in order to assist them in spreading the truth.

Discipline

[9] I have written a note to the Church, but Diotrephes, who loves to pose as a leader, refuses to receive us. If I come, I shall have to call attention to his conduct in spreading evil rumours about us. Not satisfied with that, he not only refuses to offer hospitality himself to the brethren, but those who are ready to offer it he forbids and expels them from the Church.

[11] My friend, never imitate a bad example, but only a good. He who does good is on God's side; he who does evil has never

seen God. As for Demetrius, everybody has borne testimony to him, including the Truth itself. I add my own testimony, and you know it is true.

Farewell

[13] I had a good deal to say to you, but I would rather not do it with pen and ink. I hope to see you very soon and to tell you everything by word of mouth.

Peace be with you. Your friends send their greetings. Give my kind regards to each one of mine individually.

II Peter

The authenticity of the second letter that goes by the name of S. Peter has been doubted by Christian scholars at least from the beginning of the third century (Origen). It is, however, possible that it contains actual fragments from some otherwise unknown writing of the Apostle, for example, the eye-witness account of the Transfiguration (i. 16, 17) and the prediction of his own death (cf. S. John xxi. 18, 19).

In substance, the letter is little more than a fresh edition of the Epistle of Jude. It was probably written on the outbreak of some subversive teaching similar to that castigated in the earlier writing. A new element, however, on this occasion was a denial of the Second Coming. It is in order to meet this latter danger that the author uses the authority of S. Peter, as in meeting Antinomianism he uses the arguments of S. Jude.

II Peter

I

A letter from Simon Peter, slave and apostle of Jesus Christ, to those who, through the goodness of our God and Saviour Jesus Christ, have been privileged to share with me the gift of faith:

Grace and peace be yours in abundance through this fresh knowledge of God and our Lord Jesus Christ.

Spiritual Progress

[3] Through knowing Him who has invited us to share His own honour and glory we have been made recipients by the Divine Power of everything that promotes life and piety. By the same means He has promised us great and valuable blessings, in order that you should escape the corruption that lust has brought into the world and become partakers of the Divine nature.

[5] For this very reason you must be up and doing. In addition to faith, you must supply moral excellence; and to moral excellence you must add knowledge; and to knowledge self-control, and to self-control endurance, and to endurance piety, and to piety benevolence towards fellow-members, and to such benevolence universal love. If these characteristics are abundantly displayed by you, they will ensure that you are neither idle nor unfruitful in respect of the knowledge of our Lord Jesus Christ. But he who does not possess these virtues is blind, or if he is not totally blind, he is at least short-sighted, showing himself oblivious of the fact that in baptism his old sins have been washed away. Don't you be like that, my brothers, but take pains to keep your place among God's called and chosen. If you do that you will never stumble, but will be richly endowed for your triumphal entry into the eternal kingdom of our Lord and Saviour, Jesus Christ.

Purpose of the Letter

[12] I shall always be ready to remind you of these truths, although you know them and are well grounded in the truth so far. But I consider it right, so long as I am on this side of the grave, to keep you thoroughly aroused by such reminders, knowing that I myself shall soon have to fold my tent and depart. Our Lord Jesus Christ has already given me a warning to that effect. I will do my utmost to see that after my death you will be able to recollect these reminders whenever necessary.

The Transfiguration

[16] We were not telling you a lot of fairy stories when we taught you about the manifestation of the power of our Lord Jesus Christ, but we were actually eye-witnesses of that revelation of His Majesty. Honour and glory were conferred upon Him by God the Father, when the voice spoke to Him out of the magnificent Cloud of Glory, 'This is my beloved Son in whom I take great pleasure.' That voice I myself heard coming out of Heaven when I was with Him in the sacred mountain.

The Word of Prophecy

[19] In this way we have been made more certain than ever of the fulfilment of prophecy. You had better give close attention to the prophetic sayings. They are like a night-light shining in the darkness till the day dawns and the morning star rises in your hearts. And take this as a fundamental principle, that no prophecy in Scripture is to be interpreted by private caprice but by authority. For no such prophecy ever came to us at human bidding, but men spoke as they were moved by the Holy Spirit.

II

False Teachers

There were false prophets in Israel and there will be false teachers amongst ourselves. They will introduce destructive heresies by stealth; they will even disown the Master who redeemed them; and so they will bring on themselves swift ruin. They will be immoral in their conduct, and they will attract many followers who will deride our true way of life. They will also be avaricious; and with their plausible arguments they will exploit you for gain. But their doom has long since gone forth, and destruction is ready to pounce upon them.

Warning from Previous Judgments

[4]   If God did not spare the angels when they sinned, but threw them into hell and put them in chains of darkness to be kept for the Judgment; and if He did not spare the ancient world when He overwhelmed the ungodly with a flood, protecting only Noah, the preacher of righteousness, with seven others; and if He condemned the cities of Sodom and Gomorrha to utter annihilation and turned them to ashes, giving the ungodly an example of what was in store for them and rescuing only righteous Lot who was badly upset by the licentious conduct of the lawless community (for while he lived among them the eyes and ears of that good man were assaulted day after day by their lawlessness); if God did all this, then He knows both how to rescue the godly out of their trials and also how to keep the bad under punishment till the Day of Judgment, especially those who follow a debased manner of life in the defilement of lust and scornfully defy constituted authority.   Undisciplined fire-eaters as they are, they do not hesitate to slander dignitaries whether natural or supernatural, against whom even the angels, though greater in power and authority, dare bring no slanderous charge before the Lord.

[12]   But they, just like brute beasts who are lured to destruction through their need to satisfy their natural appetite, shall be brought to utter destruction by the very forces they so ignorantly abuse; and they will make a bad bargain out of their wickedness. Such are the men who think it real pleasure to go carousing in the day time.   They are blots and blemishes on society, using their very love-feasts as an opportunity for revelling, even when you are at the feast with them.   Everything they see arouses lascivious thoughts and leads them in an endless chain of sin.

They entice others who have no stability, for they are thoroughly practised in all the arts of the avaricious. They are a curse both to themselves and to others.

[15] Such men have left the straight way and strayed off from the right path. They have followed the example of Balaam the son of Beor, who loved tainted money and earned a rebuke for his misdeed; for the dumb ass spoke with a human voice and stopped the mad action of the prophet. They are as useless as dried-up springs, or as vague mists driven by the wind. Uttermost darkness awaits them in the end.

[18] With their boastful, empty claims and by their playing on low and guilty passions they entice away those who are beginning to break free from an evil environment, promising them freedom while they themselves are slaves of corruption. How true it is that a man always becomes the slave of his conqueror!

[20] As for those who have escaped the defilements of this world through their knowledge of our Lord and Saviour Jesus Christ, if they are entangled again and brought into subjection, their last state will be worse than the first. For it would have been better for them never to have known the way of righteousness than to have known it and then to have turned aside from the holy commandment delivered to them. They illustrate the truth of the proverb, 'The dog returns to its vomit, and the cleansed sow to her wallowing in the mire.'

III

The Certainty of the Last Coming

This, my friends, is the second letter I have written you. In both I have tried to arouse your yet uncontaminated minds by bringing certain points to your notice. Especially do I wish you to recall the oracles spoken of old by the holy prophets and the commandments of the Lord and Saviour delivered to you by your apostles. Only this you must bear in mind above all, that it is a sign of the Last Days when mockers come and make sport of holy things and excuse themselves for following their own passions by asking, Where is the promised Advent? and by asserting that since the first generation of Christians everything has remained just as it was in the beginning. In their wishful thinking they have forgotten that it was God's word of creation which formed the heavens of old and made the earth out of water and fixed it between the upper and lower waters. At the bidding of the same word that first world was deluged and destroyed by water. By the same word again the heaven and earth that now exist are being treasured up for destruction by fire, kept against the Day of Judgment and destruction of the ungodly.

[8] My friends, don't forget this one thing: to God a day is like a thousand years to us and a thousand years to us is like a day to Him. The reason for the apparent delay in the fulfilment of Christ's promise to come again is not due to the reasons commonly alleged by our opponents, but to the fact that God is exercising great patience towards you. He does not wish that any should be lost, but that all should be brought to repentance. The Day of the Lord will come like a thief. Then the heavens will disappear with a great hissing sound like that of fire; the stars and planets will burn themselves out and be destroyed; and the earth, with everything in it made by man, will be found no more.

Exhortation

[11] Since everything is thus in a state of dissolution, how holy and reverent ought you to be in your behaviour, while you wait and long for the coming of that Day of God when the heavens will be dissolved by fire and the heavenly bodies will melt away with burning heat. But in fulfilment of His promise we expect them to be replaced by a new heaven and a new earth. In those righteousness will have its home.

[14] So, my friends, as you live in this expectation, make it your aim to be found by Him without spot or blemish, and at peace. Remember that the patience of our Lord means salvation. That is what our beloved brother Paul wrote to you in accordance with the insight granted to him. That is the teaching he gave in all the letters in which he touched on these matters. However,

in his letters there are some difficult passages, which ignorant and unstable people twist, as they do other scriptures, to their own destruction.

[17] But you, my friends, are forewarned; and so you can be on your guard not to be carried away by the error of the wicked or to fall from your own fixed standard, but to increase in grace and in the knowledge of our Lord and Saviour Jesus Christ. His is the glory both now and in eternity.

5489-1
119